To Grace,
all my best.
C. D. Bonner

I Talk Slower
Than I Think

C. D. Bonner

DEDICATION

This collection is dedicated to my grandfather, a man who lived his life to its fullest--the farmer, mechanic, inventor, and gold miner who chased women until he fell dead into his dinner at age 89 with a big smile. It is also dedicated to my partner PJ. She has supported my efforts in many arenas for years, and she has taken on the challenges in her life with a kid's curiosity and a stubborn enthusiasm. It is dedicated to my extended family who provided encouragement and untold hours of entertainment. And it is dedicated to our elderly Basset, Flash, who taught me patience and how to pace myself.

CONTENTS

INTRODUCTION

These 52 Creative-Non-fiction stories capture some of the amusing tales and a few tragic moments we had growing up. Few people have tasted a biscuit that was so hard firemen had to remove it; ripped out their eyebrows in a quarry diving miscalculation, or been carded to purchase hemorrhoid cream. These stories remind grown-ups of simpler, more satisfying times and give adolescents a chance to discover the fun of exploring the wonders just outside their door. Although fans of Southern humor will enjoy the flavor, growing up transcends time and place. These are true stories for adults and adolescents to enjoy, but trying these things at home is at your own risk. Enjoy the stories, then grab your Granny's best tea strainer and go catch some tadpoles. Set aside the helicopter parenting and regardless of your age, go outside and play in the dirt.

1

KEEPING YOUR HALF-WITS ABOUT YOU

It's important to keep your wits about you, especially in a crisis. It's also important to keep your half-wits about you. They make you look smarter than you really are, which is especially important at election time. Barry was among the half-dozen young men who drove fast cars and chased girls with Uncle Bert when they were in their late teens. One of their occasional pastimes was sneaking over to the abandoned quarry to swim. The quarry was a dangerous place.

It had, "No Trespassing" signs for a reason. People had been crippled and killed jumping into it. But it was just a big hole in the ground not worth actually guarding. Signs and parental advice were enough for most people.

Bert, Barry and Barry's younger brother John decided to go swimming. Another carload of friends tagged along in their Mustang, following Bert's more powerful 1963 Ford Galaxie. Bert had bought the Galaxie because it was fast; it had been hopped up to haul liquor at some time in its life. At 110, your view out the windshield narrowed by half. At 130, the pavement looked like it was only six inches wide.

Bert slid to a stop not far from the quarry's edge. When he turned to check on the trailing Mustang, Barry sprang out and made a dead run for the cliff. "I'm first!" he shouted. Bert yelled back, "No! Don't!" but Barry disappeared over the edge just as the Mustang rolled to a stop.

The whole group darted to the quarry's edge. They couldn't see him, but they heard his "Ahhh!" echo across the pit. Barry's "Ahhh!" went on. And on. And on. Then it was silent. They stared at each other in horror. Maybe he was dead. John, who tended to be emotional, welled with tears and sobbed aloud. They heard a sound echo up to them. Barry was alive.

It took Barry a long time, but he managed to climb up the wall on the lower side of the quarry opposite the group. Barry had known that the quarry had two cliffs: a forty-foot side that people sometimes dove from, and a higher side people avoided. The drop from the high side was a hundred forty feet to the water. Two beers hadn't improved Barry's judgment, but he would never have jumped off the high side deliberately. He realized his mistake about ten feet down and he had another hundred thirty feet to mull it over.

I saw Barry the next day. He didn't talk much, because he was completely deaf for about a week. His redhead's complexion exaggerated his raccoon eyes. He could stand and walk, albeit stiffly and slowly. His broken nose was swollen. But Barry's eyebrows were most fascinating. They were gone. He had managed to cheat death by straightening out his dive on the way down, but the force of the water had ripped both eyebrows clean off his head. Cleaner than he could have shaved them. Slicker than a Brazilian-waxed Escalade.

When Bert brought Barry by our place, people went inside to get their Polaroid cameras. I hope Barry showed those pictures to his kids before they reached their teen years.

2

THE IMPORTANCE OF BISCUITS

Biscuits were not just a side dish growing up--they were a staple. My mother smiled and hummed while she stoked the little wood stove at four in the morning as my brother Jake and I sang our, "I Want a Biscuit" song until those hard-crust delights were laid out on the table. They weren't the fluffy kind from the breakfast bar. They were lumpy cathead biscuits made from lard and Gold Medal flour (no cats were actually harmed in the making of these biscuits). They were wonderful, but it's possible to love something too much.

The biscuits were laid out on the kitchen table with respect, the way people used to lay out their dead relatives on the their kitchen table for their wake. They would sit up all night drinking and etching their memories like scrimshaw by retelling all the funny things the deceased had been involved in.

Mother would take a stick of margarine out of the little round-topped fridge, and butter half of them while they were still too hot to eat. There would be buttered biscuits, sugar-dipped biscuits, biscuits with sorghum syrup, and biscuits with either Red-eye or Sawmill gravy. Maybe once a week, eggs or thick streak-o-lean bacon accompanied the biscuits to the table, like company from out of town.

When I was three, we moved from the little house in Stockbridge into low-income apartments on the edge of Atlanta, where my brother started school. On his third or fourth day, Mother was running far behind in her routine and the biscuits weren't ready. I was protesting loudly that I wanted a <u>biscuit</u>. On his way out the door, Jake pointed at the white porcelain outside doorknob, telling me, "There's your biscuit," as he made a dash for the big flat-nosed yellow bus.

My muffled cries couldn't be heard through the thick wood. I pounded on the door. Mother shoved the door open, nearly taking my teeth and jawbone with it. "Stop fooling around!" was all she said before yanking the door closed again, jamming my nose hard into the wooden door.

She eventually missed me, and opened the door again, gently. This time I made wild gesticulations with my muffled protests. When she saw that I had the doorknob stuck in my teeth, she went into a full mother's panic. She tried prying my mouth open, but to no avail. It was chilly, but not cold that autumn morning. Spittle drooled down my chin, and I got mad at my brother. I was calm and patient, but I didn't know what to do. I tried prying my jaws off the door with my own hands, but the doorknob was larger than my mouth and it only made my jaws ache even more. At least the doorknob was low, though I had to stand up on my toes off and on to remain comfortable.

Mother disappeared for a bit, and it was quiet until a policeman arrived in a car with its cherry light spinning but sparing us the embarrassment of the siren. I couldn't see the car, but I could see the flashing light reflected upon the door, which was all I had seen in a very long time. A couple of neighbors had joined the audience by this time, clucking and talking in hushed tones. The policeman surveyed the situation seriously. He tried prying. He considered taking the knob off the door. He called for the assistance of a fireman. The fireman told Mother he could unhinge my mouth, but it might break my jaw. She gave a worried nod, and he dug his thumbs into the corners of my jaws, pushing down, hard, and I fell free of the doorknob. I wiped the spittle off, and thanked him as best I could with a mouth numb from too much "biscuit."

That was the second-hardest biscuit I would ever have at my Mother's house.

3

TAKE A BITE OUT OF LIFE

My mother had dental problems, even in her late twenties. I don't know why or what kind, but in 1969 she had saved enough money to go to the dental school to get new teeth. She had her remaining teeth removed over several trips and had to wait for the swelling to go down before she was fitted for upper and lower plates.

We made one more trip, where they took the impressions. Then it was time for the big day, when she got her new teeth. It was on that same trip that she took us to redeem her three-year collection of S&H Green Stamps. She diligently shopped at places that displayed the squeaky swinging metal Green Stamp sign and pasted them into the books. There were several boxes of neatly completed books. Coupons were not yet in common use, but mothers everywhere pasted Green stamps like they were coveted Ration Books.

Although she'd already picked out her prize in their catalogue, she still took us up and down all the aisles of the redemption store. I'm not sure if I found redemption there or not, but it was a religious experience for her. There were rows and rows of appliances and sturdy American-made household luxury items. She picked out an Oster hair clipper set, a nice one with all kinds of attachments. The box was quite heavy for its size. She paid a dollar for the special oil to keep it properly lubricated.

In the car, she chatted excitedly about her big score. For absolutely free, she'd earned something, and she had picked something that would save the family even more money. She wasn't the kind of person who would have considered some luxury for herself. She would even skip meals when food was scarce and payday was a few days distant. We wouldn't have to pay Dr. Bartlett to cut our hair any more--the veterinarian who had a barbershop attached to his practice overlooking

5

his fishpond. My grandmother rented his old farmhouse further up the hill. Giant towers that supported main power lines straddled both structures (which may explain a lot of things.) Dr. Bartlett would still repair Granny's dogs, but now Mother could fix our hair herself. She was about equally as excited about those clippers as she was about her new teeth.

We waited in the car while they fitted her dentures. She returned to the car, flashing a big smile. She said the teeth fit well, and they were nice and straight, quite natural-looking. Those students had done a good job.

She'd had to forego a few favorite foods during the extractions and recovery. She was anxious to try out her new choppers, and there was only one target on her scope. A Butterfinger. She loved them. And she'd not been able to eat one for a long time. We stopped at a five and dime and bought her a dozen bars.

She got the first one unwrapped just as we reached Big Five Points in Atlanta, where the animated traffic cop still choreographs traffic. I hope he gets a little something extra in his retirement check. He was the same traffic cop who had smacked Uncle Dave's friend's butt with his nightstick just a few weeks earlier when he mooned him through a car window.

The Falcon station wagon eased through early afternoon light traffic. We slowed as we approached the intersection where all five streets meet, barely rolling alongside our choreographer. He was dancing, whistling and moving traffic with rapid smooth motions he'd rehearsed for a long time. I swear he was using an eight-count to do it.

Mother chomped hard into the candy bar with unfamiliar teeth. It wouldn't break. She bit harder. She tried leverage, hoping to snap it off. Nothing. She bit down hard again and pulled. The policeman's arms dropped and his eyes bulged when both her plates came out on the end of the Butterfinger. He perked up quickly to respond to the car next to us, whose driver was staring straight at my mother, and Mother was staring in cross-eyed disbelief at the teeth at the end of her nose. The cop gave his whistle a long, full breath to halt the distracted driver who had rolled into the middle of the intersection, then waved him on through.

Mother recovered, and held the toothy treat in her lap until we got through the intersection. I'm so glad she laughed first. We couldn't contain it any longer ourselves. We laughed off and on for a couple of days.

Mother practiced until she mastered eating Butterfingers with the dentures. Then she practiced with corn on the cob. After a while she could eat anything she wished. She never quite mastered the hair clippers. It was a good thing that Jake and I had developed an interest in Mohawk haircuts from watching Daniel Boone re-runs. Once, when her hand slipped, I got a Reverse Mohawk, with a wide groove down the center of my head. It grew back within a few months, but that school picture is one of my most treasured things.

We miss you, Mom.

4

WILD AND FREE

The Jackson place, where Jackson Estates sits astride Highway 138 now, was one house uphill from a small creek that flowed from a little lake. Scrub pines screened us from the houses on either side. The pines and honeysuckle tangles behind the house opened up into big fields of broom grass. There was plenty of wildlife, and some of it could kill you.

Dad caved in one Easter, buying us each a duckling from a guy taking advantage of such parents. They were noisy and smelled funny, but they were cute. At first we tried keeping them in one of the two ancient chicken houses, but they easily escaped. One by one, they fell prey to the weasels that roamed the area. We squawled as we heard them torn apart beneath our feet during the night. It was an awful noise. My Dad was able to intervene once, but he worked night security and carried our only gun with him to work. We had to retrieve the remains of one from beneath the house about once a week. Then all were gone.

Early one summer's eve, my Dad reached for the stick he used as his window prop so he could raise his bedroom window even wider. We all came running when we heard a loud bellow, the smack of a window falling to the sill, and a parade of profanity. He had calmed a bit by the time we got in there. "Snake on the windowsill," was all he said before he closed the door. When he had reached sleepily for his window prop, he'd wondered why the stick was all floppy. Black snakes make poor window props without a good taxidermist. Not many snakes get to fly, but Dad gave that one a one-way ticket from Riverdale to Jonesboro.

I was four when we moved there from the apartment. I knew outhouses from my Granny's place, so outside plumbing was no big deal. Or so I thought. I was almost to the outhouse with a Sears catalog one day when I heard my frightened Mother shout from the front porch, "Don't move!" I froze. I slowly looked up at her. "Why?" "Bobcat! Don't run!" Only then did I notice the big cat maybe five feet behind and to my left. His back legs were tallest, and they were chest level to me. His orange spotted fur was nothing like a house cat, and the tufts stuck out of his ears a lot farther. I could hear it breathing. "Walk slow, back up here. But don't run!" The big cat had been silent.

There was no way I'd have known it was there if Mother hadn't shouted. I kept one eye on it as I slowly made a wide circle up to the house. The cat didn't move. It just watched me. As I neared the porch, it lost interest and padded silently off into the woods.

"I should have run," I told Mother once we were inside. "No," she explained, tears streaming down her young face, "That makes you look like prey. Never run from one."

I was unnerved but prepared the second time the cat sneaked up on me. We learned to look out the windows before going out. If there was a bobcat roaming the yard, you just waited a while.

Ah, the things you have to teach your kids. But I didn't end up with a headstone saying, "Eaten on his way to the bathroom." And no one had to convince my teacher to accept a note saying, "Sorry that C.D. won't be in school today. He was eaten by bobcats."

5

FUNNY BONES

I come from a long line of jokers and practical jokers. It runs in the family at least back to my grandfather and his father.

Uncle Dave and Uncle Bert shared some of the same friends as teens, and when they rode around, they encouraged each other in creative but usually harmless mischief. They had a favorite intersection. It was a favorite because it was six lanes wide and on an incline. With a load of friends in each car, they would ease up to the light. They timed their arrival so that each of them reached a front position at the traffic light, leaving an unsuspecting driver between. They checked their mirrors for approaching traffic, and with a quiet nod, they pushed in their clutches, rolling quietly backwards in unison. Quite a few drivers stomped holes in their floorboards trying to stop their already stationary cars.

My Pawpaw, John, went to see a fancy traveling preacher back in the Twenties, a man of some notoriety who heavily advertised his visit before he even arrived. John listened to the preacher's fiery sermon. He was pretty good. The preacher concluded his sermon with a thinly veiled request for money, or at least groceries. He lifted his face toward the sky and proclaimed that God would send him, "A side of bacon, a sack of flour, and a pound of coffee."

John was interested enough to go again. Traveling preachers were treated like entertainers in small towns back then, with the locals grading them on their performance. He took his best friend with him to the next show. The boys were about fourteen or fifteen but were older than their years. John had been working full-time since he was twelve driving a shingle truck and assisting a moonshiner. The preacher gave the same sermon to a new crowd, with the same ending. John and his friend looked at each other and grinned.

The third night of the show, John and his friend went to the movie theater early. They carried with them a side of bacon, a cloth sack of flour, and a sack of coffee. They had seen the trap door above the stage, and that's where they lay in wait.

They slid back the trap door cover in the attic before anyone arrived and waited patiently through the whole sermon, being careful not to make any noise. When the preacher uttered, "Side of bacon!" the side of bacon fell at his feet with a wet "smack." He looked nervously out at the crowd. He hesitated a bit before saying, "Sack of flour," and it landed with a dull "thump." He sweated. When he hurriedly spat, "Pound of coffee," it dropped from above; but as soon as it hit the floor, the preacher's heels were in motion. He ran straight up the center aisle, leaving a trail of profanity that hung in the air like dust in a stable. He jumped in his car and was gone.

There were mixed reactions. Several cussed angrily. A few gave joyful thanks for a miracle. But most just held their bellies in unrestrained laughter. The preacher was never seen again.

My great-grandfather, Ben, was visiting his son, who had done well enough to build a nice brick ranch home. The son had all his relatives over for a housewarming bar-b-que to show off the new place.

Ben ate a bit and walked around, taking it all in while the younger folks talked and laughed. He returned with a somber look, and told his son earnestly, "Son, I'm glad to see that you are doing so well. I never thought any son of mine would be cooking in the yard and crapping in the house."

I sure miss that old man. People still talk about him.

6

NO CHILD LEFT BEHIND

I was very young when I heard of Fritz and Arlene's misadventure. They had traveled way out West somewhere, to Texas or Oklahoma, with a carload of kids. By a carload, I mean eight or nine and counting. I'm not certain if they went to visit family or if Fritz was waiting for another scrape with the law to cool down. He'd been in jail a few times for bad checks. Fritz was the father of Mike, my second cousin, twice (forcibly) removed.

They had herded the kids into the big Vista station wagon, the kind with an extra rear-facing seat and observation windows looking out of the roof. They'd been away from home for several weeks and were tired. Arlene was expecting, again. Somewhere out on the Texas plains they stopped to buy gas and Moon pies and let the kids overwhelm the plumbing of a Sinclair station. While they attended to their personal needs, the gas station attendant filled their tank, checked the tire pressure, topped off all the engine fluids and washed the outside of the windshield. But not the inside. For some reason people back then never washed the inside, leaving a haze of dust and cigarette residue that was sold with the car.

They were on the road and headed back toward Georgia, making decent time. Fritz heard a low whine. He mentioned to Arlene that they should have the rear axle lube checked when they got home. It often whined like that, and if you let it go, the bearings would burn out. The whine got louder. A couple of cars passed them even though they were driving the speed limit. The whining got louder as the minutes passed. Fritz' brow furrowed. A rear axle repair could be costly, and he had lots of mouths to feed.

Several more cars passed Fritz and Arlene. Despite the cherry light flashing atop his cruiser, the State Trooper had been unable to get their attention from behind the line of cars. Now that he was directly behind, he moved his car alongside theirs, motioning for them to pull over. Fritz just drove on, puzzled—he was going just under the speed limit. Finally, the Trooper pointed to the back seat of the police car. Fritz' son Randall's face was pushed hard against the glass, his face red and puffy from crying.

The Trooper fussed at Fritz for a good ten minutes. "How could you not know you'd left a kid in the bathroom? I've been chasing you for two hundred miles!" He surveyed the situation, but none of the other kids looked neglected. A couple of them calmly made baloney sandwiches while the Trooper lectured Fritz and Arlene. He accepted their explanation of too many heads to count. With a stern warning, he turned his cruiser back the way he'd come.

Fritz and Arlene were a little chagrined, but not as much as you'd expect. When I heard them tell the story at our house in Georgia, Fritz was focused on his irritation with the Trooper. I concluded that it must be easy to lose a kid when you have a third of a classroom of kids scattered around a gas station. And I suspected Fritz and Arlene felt they had kids to spare.

When my parents visited family or friends, they wouldn't just get into the car for the return trip. There were at least two rounds of, "I guess we have to head home" comments, sometimes three or four. If they were in a hurry, there was a ten-minute space between the first comment and putting the key into the ignition. Kids had to be emptied; heads had to be counted. When the group we visited was larger, the three or four rounds of parting remarks would take a half-hour to forty-five minutes.

After hearing of Fritz and Arlene leaving a kid behind, I always made sure I was first into the car. I wasn't entirely convinced they'd left Randall in that gas station bathroom accidentally. He could be an unpleasant kid. I wondered if I'd done enough bad things to be left behind. I never got into anything truly bad, but the small uncertainty nagged at me enough that I claimed my seat in the car early. Sometimes I slept, other times I just let my mind wander.

No one was leaving me behind.

7

YOU CAN'T CRACK ONE PECAN

As I stand this cool wet morning listening to the bacon frying on the pecan leaves and upon macadam pavement that walks by the front door, I remember my grandfather's advice, "You can't crack one pecan." The pace here in our little Alabama town is too slow for that road to run by here. It can take its time to walk by at a steady pace and wave at the neighbors as it passes by. It knows all 1431 of us by name. It has known our names since it was laid down in front of this house in 1885--generations of names who lived, moved in and out, and passed on.

"Pick it up and put it into your pocket," Pawpaw told me one day when I was five. I had kicked a single pecan from the scant droppings that hot, dry year. I dutifully did, but wondered to myself what I was going to do with just one. It was not enough to eat.

Soon he picked up a single nut and dropped it into a pocket of his Bibb overalls. When we reached the corner of the yard opposite the chicken coop and the place where the two scary peacocks lived, we found perhaps a dozen more.

"Keep your last pecan in your pocket, and you won't go hungry this time of year," he said as he cracked one pecan against the other, working carefully around the sides until he slipped the shell apart, leaving two full, tasty halves. "See that leather between the halves, and stuck in the grooves? That's really bitter." He handed me the pecan to clean. I missed cleaning a bit of leather between the halves, and I wasn't able to get it all out of the grooves. When I ate the nut, it dried my mouth like an unripe persimmon. He laughed at the face I made.

It was a while before I developed the hand strength to crack pecans properly. My brother and sister and I gathered bushels of them when we lived at the back of the 40-acre farm Pawpaw rented. We used rocks and claw hammers to duplicate the cracking technique as best we could. The meat was rich and earthy tasting, and you could just pick them up by the bagful in a good year. But some years, the trees wouldn't bear anything except the occasional green snake.

We were poor kids living a rich life. That forty-acre spot was more magical than Christopher Robin's Hundred Acre Wood. Many things grew wild, and other things Pawpaw planted. Depending on the season, we looked forward to gorging on small wild plums the size of nickels; on a half-acre of strawberries; on blackberries the size of our little thumbs. Sometimes we would just explore and talk and eat that season's offerings. Other times we would gather most of it up for my Granny to do something magical in the kitchen. Freshly picked purple, thick-hulled muscadine grapes went in, and delicious preserves came out of that kitchen—the kind with the hulls left in. The same fate awaited figs, pears and apples.

We grew up on a diet of fresh beans and greens with a little fatback bacon or sausage that complemented the hard crust cat-head biscuits she made from scratch (no real cats were harmed during the making of these biscuits). We had no money for store-bought treats, but we awoke each morning eager to explore the bounty around us. Granny told us to, "Go catch me four turtles, big ones, and I'll make you turtle soup. But you have to find four." We were off in a shot.

We had never tasted turtle soup, but it sounded good, even exotic. There were two edges of the farm that bordered a small swamp. Our senses were sharpened as we hunted those turtles, using fresh cut cane poles to poke around, since we sometimes flushed a black snake from beneath the grass--which only added to our excitement. It took us two or three days to find four turtles of suitable size. Once we had, we watched her prepare the soup then played outside while it cooked. It was quite good, served up with Oyster Crackers. Other times she would send us for a half-dozen green frogs (never toads) that had to be "this big" for a treat of frog's legs. It was thirty years before I appreciated her tactic to get noisy kids out of the house all day.

Being the youngest, I trotted behind my Pawpaw many days, asking a million questions. He was greatly amused that I would listen, then come back late in the day, giving my annoyed explanation *why* something he told me just to stop my questioning could not possibly be true. Then he would take the time to give a proper answer to any question, and I would soak it all in.

I was three or four when I began walking close on his heels, asking how everything in the world worked of this old, wise man who could do just about anything. It is sobering to realize that I have reached that same age and am not half as wise.

I have one pecan in my pocket this morning. It was still dark when I opened the wooden screen door, and I cracked it a little when I stepped on it. Last night's storm blew it onto the porch. What a wonderful place to live, where pecans are delivered to your doorstep.

8

EUREKA

Both my grandfathers were bright, inquisitive men. My Grandpa Stacks held patents on the Rumble Seat and some specialized concrete blocks. He kept a Stanley Steamer automobile going during World War Two when gasoline was hard to get. Pawpaw Bonner's approach was less formal, but his unorthodox solutions came more frequently. I think his response to obstacles sprang from the mountain isolation and lack of financial resources in his youth.

My father was about six when the brakes went out on top of a mountain five miles from nowhere. Considering neighbors were a mile or more apart in their district, "five miles from nowhere" carried a lot of weight. This was serious. Pawpaw turned to my Dad, "Give me a shoe." My Dad stared in disbelief. He wasn't sure what his new shoes could solve, and shoes were rationed during the War. Pawpaw saw his hesitance and added, "I just need one of the tongues." Dad used his pocketknife to cut a tongue from one shoe. Pawpaw carefully cut a perfect circle of leather. He slipped the new leather seal into the bore of the brake master cylinder, and once they'd filled it with brake fluid and bled out the air, they were safely on their way.

Pawpaw was grinning over the scattered parts of Granny's old sewing machine when I stopped by one day. The headliner in his car was falling out. He already had several yards of nice corduroy and he said the old headliner was intact enough to use as a pattern. I watched him modify the mechanical foot pedal sewing machine. He attached a pulley to it and found a rubber drive belt that would turn it. Once he mounted the motor from an electric grinder, he had a sewing machine tough enough to handle the thick material. Finally, he surmounted the biggest problem: getting the foot pedal that started and stopped the machine to respond properly.

He took his headliner trim off and slipped out the bows that held it against the car's roof. He carefully unstitched the five pieces of cloth and traced them onto his new material. When he finished sewing, he slipped the bows into the pockets and friction fit the headliner against the inside of the roof, then reinstalled the trim. It looked as good as a factory job. It had taken him two days but it had cost him nothing and he got professional results.

Pawpaw had a 1948 Gibson tractor my Dad bought him back in the Fifties. It was small and simple but it had a lot of pulling power for a single-cylinder nine horsepower tractor. It was built with a tiller instead of a steering wheel. You started it with a rope, and it had a distinctive sputtering sound that I will always associate with Pawpaw.

By 1975, the intake and exhaust valves had worn out in the Gibson. Before the Internet, such parts were impossible to find. Pawpaw got up early one morning and gathered what he needed. Two bags of coal. A bag of coke (the kind you burn to make steel). An old bar-b-que grill. Hammers and files. A micrometer.

After two weeks of slow, careful hammering and filing he had new valves. Considering that the stem must be absolutely dead-centered to the flat face of the valves, this was a fine accomplishment. He met accuracy tolerances of ten-thousandths of an inch—about the thickness of a cigarette paper—and he made them without power tools. Those valves were still working when Pawpaw passed away eighteen years later.

I am stubborn, but not as creative as Pawpaw. I've done a few small things, such as adapting plumbing parts to my Studebaker. The reproduction water pump's fittings were smaller than the original, and I had to find a way to match the different water fitting diameters. I guess the spirit is there, but without a farm to care for there are fewer jobs that require me to hone those skills.

In the area where Pawpaw grew up in Alabama, such attitudes persist. Skills are at least as respected as money or formal education. There is a strong tradition of self-sufficiency driven by economics, geographic isolation, and pride. Even well off people are looked down upon as wasteful when they pay others to do work they are physically able to do or capable of learning. The customer base is small in a state whose entire population is about half that of New York City. Alabamans adapt by diversifying, with many people doing three or four different things. Despite the challenges, people seem to be more satisfied here. Seeing the direct results of your own labor has a lot to do with your satisfaction level.

I still miss both my grandfathers. I may not be able to pass along all their skills, but I will do my best to pass along their problem-solving approaches.

9

SNAKE BITE

I was about two, my brother Jake about three, when we moved from the community of Stonewall to a pretty white house in Stockbridge. The house sat just behind a mom and pop store--the kind with straight chairs out front and a hoop of cheese on the counter next to the sticks of baloney and penny candy. A big church now sits where our house once was.

We had only been there a short time. Dad had promised to take us fishing the following Saturday and we were trying to gather bait. It was rather dry, and we only turned up two or three night crawlers from beneath the pine needles at the edge of the yard.

Jake figured that there should be plenty in the dirt beneath the house. It was cool under there, and dark. It was approaching dusk when he decided to go through the access door. He carried our only flashlight. I would have joined him, but I had no light of my own, and it was spooky under there. I hung back, just outside the door.

Jake came back with a tin can of worms and nicks all over his legs. "They bite," he said. I'd never heard of biting worms before, but I accepted it. He took the can into the house. Before he could put it away, Mother let out a loud wail. Jake had found a nest of snakes and mistaken the small ones for worms. He'd been bitten numerous times.

Dad rushed Jake to the family doctor in our little English Ford. It was serious. The doctor said there was nothing he could do and phoned Dixon's Funeral Home to dispatch their ambulance. The nearest hospital of any size was Grady, at least a half an hour away. The driver loaded Jake into the back, but before he took off, he paused to pack Jake's legs in ice. It was going to be a long ride.

It was dark when Bert and my Dad came back to the house. They opened the access door carefully, and Bert went under with a forked stick and a lantern. He returned after a few minutes with a couple of small snakes and a bigger one, probably the mother. They said that the hospital had stabilized Jake, but hey were unable to administer the right anti-venom until we determined what kind of snake they were dealing with.

Jake didn't return for several days, and I missed him. I was worried about him. He'd had a rough go of it his first couple years. He'd been in the hospital with pneumonia for two weeks and nearly died. It was so bad that Mother called Billy Graham, who flew in to pray at the bedside. It was more like giving last rites, but Jake recovered.

His next close call was at the old hotel we lived in. It sat next to the railroad tracks in Riverdale, across from the hardware store. Nearly a century after General Sherman's urban renewal project passed it by, the three-story wooden structure was dilapidated. I was almost a year old, in diapers and still learning to talk, but that place left an impression on me. There were rats. Big ones. Brown ones, black and white ones, and grey ones. With attitude. They would hiss at you like possums from numerous holes in the walls. Lying on the bed with the adults talking in the next room, I was petrified. It felt like the rats were shaking the bedsprings and mattress, but it could just as easily have been my heartbeat shaking the bed.

The structure was falling apart, too. Jake crawled out onto the balcony that had been cordoned off. I don't know how he got the door open, but he was out there on rotten planks too weak to support any adult who tried to rescue him. Finally, Mother got him interested in a broom as a toy. He latched on, and she yanked him back across the gaps in the floorboards to safety.

Jake came home from Grady after a week or two. He was weakened, but he had survived the snakebites. They'd given him a total of twenty-one injections of anti-venom. He had been bitten by an obscure species not even native to the US. It took a while, but we eventually found out that a man just down the road raised exotic snakes, including poisonous ones.

I'm still close to my only brother. We've been through a lot together, and we've both survived some hard times and close calls. I want to thank that ambulance driver, publicly, for going beyond what was expected of him. Packing the little kid in ice had been his own initiative, and slowing down Jake's circulation saved him. In those days, ambulance drivers were exactly that—drivers. Most had little or no first aid training. Many moonlighted using a hearse from a local funeral home. Mother called Dixon after things settled down, and the driver took the time to come over see Jake. He and Mother exchanged relieved looks and beaming smiles.

10

CAUGHT STEALING

The little house in Stockbridge was one of the nicest places I remember living. It was a simple white frame house with high concrete steps leading to the front door. It sat in the triangle where Highway 138 departs Stockbridge on its way to Conyers. Only a patch of milkweed separated our front door from the old store wedged into the fork of the road. Jake and I weren't allowed to go all the way to the store, but we did play at the edge of the milkweed, a plant we studied with great interest.

The house was nice and we were making ends meet. Dad was a truck driver, hauling local loads around Atlanta and working the loading docks. He only occasionally made a long-haul run with a big rig. Mother got a job welding and bending pipe at a muffler shop. She earned enough money to buy a compact car, a little English Ford Prefect. It resembled a yellow and white potato. I remember feeling the rain sting my hands that I stuck out the window on the way back from Grant Park Zoo. We would visit the zoo to admire Willie B. the gorilla and meet up with Mother's sister at the A&W drive-in for a milkshake afterwards. The Kennedy years were good to us.

We had a young Basset hound named Sammy. He loved kids and we enjoyed playing with him. He spent most of his time indoors with us, but would do a little exploring. One day, Dad sat on the orange vinyl couch watching TV. A woman was irritated and shouting something. Her shrill noise was getting closer to him--never a good sign. It was like having a police siren approaching your house, but you don't know why they are coming. This couldn't be good.

He reached the door in time to see Sammy running up the trail through the milkweed, his long ears swinging. Sammy had the end of a full stick of baloney clenched between his teeth, and he struggled to run with it trailing between his short legs. The sweaty, rotund lady huffing and puffing after him on her own short legs had shorter ears.

Sammy had scored a stick his own approximate size and shape, and he wasn't about to surrender it. My Dad was still chasing Sammy around the house to pry the baloney loose when the storeowner caught up, arriving in a cloud of steam. She was livid.

Dad walked down the slope to the store with the baloney tucked under his arm to make amends. Sammy straggled just behind, growling. Although Dad tried to do the right thing, the owner was uncooperative. Dad offered to pay her for the damaged end of the stick, but she demanded he buy the whole thing. He argued that the delivery guy had left the baloney outside on the store's front porch, and that dogs will act as dogs do. My Dad lost the heated argument and had to pay fifteen dollars for the baloney--a couple of days' pay. We ate baloney at every meal for a long time.

Our friend Sammy disappeared soon afterwards, under suspicious circumstances. I wonder if she was still mad about the baloney.

11.

KEEPING ME IN STITCHES

Mother took my older sister Doris, Jake and me on a picnic in the country. We were excited. She loaded us into the blue and white '57 Ford station wagon. It was a monster, with a hood that opened backwards. We drove several miles to Mundy's Mill, an old mill that became famous when Margaret Mitchell used it in her book, "Gone With the Wind." We had been there once before and had been very impressed with the splashing water wheel and old building.

The road leading from Highway 54 to the mill was dirt then. You had to cross a small plank bridge to reach it. As Mother unpacked the car, we wandered around exploring. We peeked through the planks of the bridge, watching the water flow by. Maybe we'd see some fish.

Doris and Jake picked blackberries from the bank of the road. I walked the road's edge on the opposite side. It had rained recently and the big yellow Caterpillar belly scrapers hadn't scraped the ditches for a while. They were filled almost to road level with sand. We were, of course, barefoot. We normally were in warm weather.

Coke bottles were built to be sturdy. In the days before steel-belted radial tires, people swerved to avoid a piece of bottle lying in the road. It could easily shred a nylon bias tire, which didn't have a long life expectancy anyway. The part most certain to do harm was the bottom. When some idiot tossed one onto a road, the bottle shattered into curved shards, leaving the bottom intact with a dagger-like triangle attached. I found one.

As I walked along looking for shiny rocks that might contain gold, I was careful where I stepped. It didn't help. As I stepped on the spongy sand in the ditch, I felt a sting. When I lifted my foot, a Coke bottle bottom came with it. I cried for Mother to come take it out. Mother paled. The bottle shard had gone nearly through my foot. When she

25

slid it out of the wound, blood shot a couple of feet in long pulses. It wasn't good.

She threw us into the car. It was a long way to any hospital, probably forty-five minutes. She drove quickly toward the main road. Before we reached the paved road, she saw a lady standing in her side yard alongside the dirt road. She whipped the car into their driveway and leapt out, explaining the situation. Mother asked where the nearest hospital was, but the lady replied that I wouldn't make it to any hospital once she had examined my foot. "Bring him inside."

Mother and the lady seemed calm. They carried me inside. We passed through the living room to the kitchen. I was small, so it wasn't difficult to hold me over the kitchen sink to wash the sand out the wound. It stung. She sat me on the table, telling Mother to keep my leg up high, and to keep pressure on the cut.

The lady hummed as she prepared. She found some peroxide and a sewing needle, one of medium size. She grabbed a Coke bottle and bent the needle around the neck, curving it. She poured alcohol on the needle and ran it through a candle flame a couple of times, then more alcohol. She had a soothing voice, "Hold still, child, this is gonna hurt. It won't hurt too long, but if we don't fix it, you gonna die. If you hold real still, it won't hurt as much."

Yes, it hurt. When I visit the doctor today, they ask me to rate my pain on a scale of one to ten. This would be the scale to measure against for at least the next fifty years. Mother took a firm grip. It couldn't have been easy to hold me down, but she managed, tears streaming. The old lady cooed and hummed. "This won't take long. But it will hurt for just a little while." She wasn't nervous, and she never broke a sweat. I clenched my teeth and tried to be as still as I could. But each time the needle entered, my foot involuntarily jerked.

She finished the sixth and final stitch, snipping the thread off with her scissors. She washed the wound over the sink with peroxide, which didn't sting much; then with alcohol, which stung badly. She had bloodied three of her best towels.

A teary and sweaty Mother thanked the lady profusely. The bleeding had stopped. I was going to make it. Mother loaded us into the car and she drove us to Dr. Spivey. His family owned a peach orchard that would eventually become a recreation destination when they improved their lake with a swimming beach and paved the entire perimeter of the lake for roller-skating. He was a nice doctor. I liked him.

He examined the wound carefully. He rinsed it with alcohol, which didn't sting much now, and bandaged it with gauze. "She did a fine job. I don't really have to do anything. Just keep an eye on it and come back if it swells or turns red." He gave her a bottle of penicillin liquid just in case.

I never knew the name of the lady who sewed me up in the spring of 1964. I passed through once as an adult, intending to stop and thank her if she is still alive. I was only moderately sure I saw the right house. I wasn't sure enough to stop and ask, but I will try again this year. The house was between the plank bridge and Fayetteville Road, on the right, not long before you reached the highway. I want to thank her for making a lifetime of things possible for a little redheaded kid.

12

WE GET NEW HATS

I was three and Jake was maybe five. It was a rainy day at the Blair Village apartments near the old Lakewood Fairgrounds. We watched cartoons and got interested in the characters in a Dick Tracy cartoon about missing fortune cookies. They had funny hats. Still, we were bored. Boredom would lead us to trouble.

We drew and colored for a while but were still antsy. The pent-up energy of two young boys was building and there wasn't a good way to burn it off. We rifled the house looking for something new to play with.

We found two round foam-rubber things on the dresser, about the size of saucers with little points in the middle. They were sort of dome-shaped like a hat. We put them on our heads. They were just big enough to cover our heads, and we sat around doing our best imitations of the cartoon characters. Mother laughed and didn't fuss.

The rain slacked to a drizzle. It was warm outside, and the sun shone through at times. But it was still raining. We needed rain hats. Jake took a pair of scissors and cut a small slot on the side of each foam pad. He tucked an end of a large rubber band into each slot then tied the end off in a knot. Our hats now had chinstraps.

Mother was busy cooking. We eased out the door. We splashed back and forth on the sidewalk between rows of apartments, deliberately stomping on the clear shallow water that collected on the sidewalk. The flying droplets made rainbows in the sunshine. We were thoroughly soaked. Neighbors were starting to come home from work. Some smiled. Several gave a hearty belly laugh.

Mother stuck her head out of the green wooden screen door. She got hopping mad. First, we'd gotten soaking wet. Second, we were wearing her Falsies on our heads for the amusement of all the neighbors. The light rain quickly became a storm.

She stripped them off our heads and wrung them out. They were soaked through. It would take them days to dry. She took us by the ears and marched us home on our tiptoes. Since we hadn't understood what all the fuss was about, we didn't get into real trouble. She explained that the hats were actually the pads for her brassiere, and that we had embarrassed her. We felt bad, and promised never to wear them again.

Thus began our quest to find out more about brassieres. As we matured, we found out that some were padded; some were not. Some had only one hook; some had three or four. When I reached my teens I discovered that the ones most difficult to remove were the ones equipped with a time lock that lasted eighteen hours. Locksmiths and safecrackers had trouble opening them. Fathers of teenage girls paid a premium for those.

13

WE MISS YOU, BECKY

I used to like mushroom soup. Mother would mix the skinny can with water and serve it up. Occasionally she burned it. Mother was a dear lady, but she could burn a pot of soup. But I lost my taste for mushroom soup one day when Becky came over to play.

Mother would occasionally baby-sit Becky, the daughter of one of Dad's co-workers. Although she was our age, she was stocky and much stronger. She showed no restraint when she hugged you, and you had to gasp, "Let go, you're squeezing too hard!" before she would release her grip with a broad genuine smile.

Mother told us that Becky was "different," and that she didn't understand her own strength. Even at three or four years old, I understood what Mother meant by, "Not quite right, but she is so sweet." She was. When Becky played with us, it was full steam. She was generous with all of her toys. Becky was fun to be around.

It was cold outside, so we all played in the apartment. Mother asked Becky what she wanted for lunch, knowing that Becky would announce, "Mushroom soup!" Mother cooked up a big batch and presented the steaming bowls with Oyster Crackers. Oyster crackers were reserved for company and special occasions. Becky had a bad cold. She often did, since her mother didn't pay much attention to how Becky was dressed. I guess she was distracted with her two rambunctious older children.

Her older kids were loud and obnoxious. They had a mean streak, too. I once was sitting in the living room of their little frame house when I was startled by a grey streak that was followed by the two older kids at a dead run. The rooms were laid out funny, and the kids ran in a circle from room to room chasing the cat they had shaved to its skin, except for a lion's mane and a ball on its tail. You could see its ribs and its lumpy insides. As young as I was, I thought it was mean and stupid. The poor cat had to be cold, even in the spring weather.

Doris, Jake and I sat at the table talking and laughing with Becky as we ate. Becky's nose was running into her bowl of mushroom soup. I was polite, knowing that Becky "wasn't quite right." I shifted in my chair and looked away when I could. We knew it wasn't her fault and that she didn't realize there was a problem. We grit our teeth and got through the meal, then we went back to playing.

Pneumonia took Becky not long afterward. She had wandered outside and played in the cold wet yard for hours before her mother went to look for her. She died young, a sweet girl with the purest heart of anyone I've ever known.

We miss you, Becky. Your life was short, but you are not forgotten. I'd like to tell you that you were "just right." I am among many who envy your unrestrained belly laugh and unfettered displays of affection. If you were here, I'd have mushroom soup with you.

14

BIG GROCERIES

When we lived in the apartments, I'd accompany Mother on her shopping trips. Down the hill and to the right was a small supermarket that sat down in a bowl alongside a small creek. It was small by today's standards, maybe six aisles, but it met all our needs. But to a three-year-old whose mind wandered, it was a cavern to get lost in.

She always worked counter-clockwise from the main entrance. There were two checkout lines right at the front door, and a manager's office alongside whose wall only went halfway to the ceiling. The public address system was run from his office.

We would pass the clerks clicking busily away on the mechanical cash registers and circle around his office, picking up a few fresh vegetables. By the time we got halfway up the next aisle, Mother would be gone. Vanished while my imagination took me somewhere else. I would break out into a sweat. What if she'd left? Did she remember she'd brought me on this trip? A distant cousin, once (forcibly) removed had left one of her eight kids in a gas station bathroom recently, and the State Patrol had to chase them for two hundred miles before they caught up to them with the kid.

I would walk as quickly as my short legs could carry me, trying to catch up. Nothing. It was only a block and a half--not far past the drugstore on the corner where we'd get banana splits, but I'd surely get run over if I tried to walk home. I'd end up like the kid on the news who was mashed between the tandem wheels of the school bus. They had to take the wheels off the bus to unwrap him from the axle.

The first couple of times I got sweaty and bawled until I got hiccups. The manager came over and said some soft words as he led me to the office. It happened a lot. He would pick up the public address microphone and describe the found redheaded kid. Mother would arrive soon after, and I'd stick close by for the rest of the trip. But I'd do it again the next time. I had the typical attention span of a young boy, and there were plenty of distractions around me and inside my own head.

After the third or fourth time, I just sighed and surrendered at the manager's office. I eventually asked if I could just make my own announcements, but he said with a smile that he'd rather do it.

It was the most crowded place we went. The drugstore was small, and there were only a few customers at any one time, even at the lunch counter. There might be three or four people in the coin laundry when we went to "wash rats" as she called it after I mispronounced Washer-Ette. It was a better place to daydream than the supermarket. It was boring, and I'd think about things I'd seen on The Outer Limits or other fanciful shows and make up my own stories.

Mother would forage for dried beans mostly. Potatoes. Flour and lard for the cathead biscuits. Raisin oatmeal when they had it. Maybe once a month she'd buy a large tray of cheap cookies that were expected to last.

It was rare to see a kid pitch a fit for some such treat in the store, but one time I saw a kid throw a fit and get what he wanted by stomping and screaming to embarrass his mother. It might work for me, too, I thought.

I stomped my feet like he did, loudly making a demand for some cookies. My eyes scrunched together. I wanted to make a loud public scene that Mother would cave in for. It was a bad move. Her bottom lip stuck out. She spun me around right at the beginning of the checkout line and gave me four swats on the behind. The swats didn't hurt, but the surprise and humiliation of being chastised in front of several other approving parents did. My squawling ceased with the second swat. My face burned with embarrassment.

My acting career was mercifully short. I'd grossly underestimated the united parental front. There was sympathy, but it was Mother who was receiving it. It was the one and only time I acted up like that.

15

FINALITY

I suppose we took fewer serious risks as kids because we understood the finality of death. We witnessed it from an early age, beginning with Granny killing and cleaning a chicken for a Sunday dinner with the preacher. We were disappointed that we could no longer visit her mother, Mama Butler, after she had passed on. But we understood that dead meant you weren't coming back; we had no video games to tell us otherwise.

Doris had been in school a couple of years already, but Jake had just begun first grade. The news gave graphic accounts of how a little boy ducked under a school bus to pick up something. They had to take the wheels off the bus to unwind him from the space between the tandem tires. It wasn't sensational journalism; it was a cautionary tale to kids and parents, like the safety tips printed on the back of our report cards.

To make sure we didn't make the same mistake, Dad took all of us down to the place the bus parked and showed us its tandem tires, and he described what happened to the kid. It had its desired effect. I had a healthy respect for those wheels, knowing how narrow that gap was. I guess it sunk in, because I ran into Doris many years later showing a "poor man's Frisbee" to her daughter: a cat that had met misfortune on the street that ran close alongside her house. Flat as a tortilla baked crispy in the Georgia sun. Cruel as it seemed, cars sped past her front steps at over forty miles an hour, and her toddling daughter had begun walking at just ten months old.

There were also the fatalities associated with Atlanta's expansion in the mid-Sixties. Old houses were being moved out of town for an airport expansion. I don't know where they went, but we saw many of those houses float past the apartments on unseen wheels. They rode through at a walking pace, taking up all the traffic lanes. The guys sitting on top of them would grin and wave at the kids. They sat astride the roof peak to lift the live power lines over the house. Some used a stick; others used their hands to lift the wires up and over their heads. I never saw one killed, but Uncle Dave did. I can recall four or five news stories of their deaths, but there were probably more. I guess someone paid them good money for their risk, or paid the right people not to notice.

At Pawpaw's farm, we saw rats he had poisoned to keep them out of the corncrib and small animals in the woods. But it really came home when we saw the ice cream man.

Our ice cream man owned his own truck. He had a uniform of his own choosing with a jacket and a hat like filling station attendants and bus drivers wore. My Dad wore a hat like that when he drove a truck. We would begin begging Mother for dimes as soon as we heard the music several streets behind us. Kids would come running from all over the apartment complex to meet the ice cream truck when it turned in at the bottom of the hill two rows below us. It was easier to turn around on the broad parking lot where the school buses collected and deposited kids.

I was four and Jake was five. We pried a dime apiece from Mother and trotted down the hill, cutting through two rows of apartments. I had a silver dime with a winged lady on the front.

There were six or eight kids hovering around the truck as he busily filled orders. When there was a larger crowd he made us form a neat line, but this time we were just gathered in a bunch close alongside the truck. The music played on. One kid asked for an ice cream, but when he went to pay for it, the boy looked at his empty hands in disbelief. The ice cream man made a sad face and put the ice cream back, telling him he needed a dime. The kid welled up in tears and ran off, over to the row of apartments at the foot of the hill. He trotted across a grass median and over his narrow front lawn to where his father sat drinking beer on the porch.

My attention was mostly focused on a dime that lay underneath the truck. I didn't know where it had come from, but if no one claimed it I was planning to pick it up once the truck moved.

Things just kind of exploded. A very angry man cursed, and we turned toward where the kid had run. "Nobody is going to cheat *my* son!" he bellowed between snarls of profanity. Before we could even react, he sprang off the porch and ran straight at the truck, much faster than one would expect of a drunk. Kids moved back just a couple of few feet, anticipating an argument. The ice cream man was exposed to the father's full fury.

"You cheated my son!" he spat, and with one swift motion, he raised a butcher knife from alongside his thigh and cut the throat of the ice cream man, who had no chance to explain anything. He just gurgled. The father had sliced his neck deep, laying the meat open. The ice cream man fell back into the truck bleeding. The angry father stomped off and sat back on his porch. We squealed and ran. We told mother what had happened to the ice cream man, and I mentioned the stray dime beneath the truck. I wondered if the kid had dropped it. I would never know for sure.

We followed Doris down there a bit later. The truck was still there, and the police were taking an even drunker father off that porch. We couldn't get close enough to tell anyone about the dime beneath the truck. Now he really slurred when he shouted about the expletive ice cream man who cheated his son out of a dime. They handcuffed him and stuffed him into a police car. Someone had already shut off the ice cream man's music.

It was final. The ice cream man never came back. No other ice cream man ever took his place. My Dad ran into his daughter about ten years ago near Gratis. The family still has his truck.

We miss you, ice cream man. You were nice, and fifty years later you are still remembered by the kids you were nice to.

16

BUTTER

Mother married young, and only learned to cook after she divorced. She once made biscuits that were so hard we couldn't eat them at all. We played baseball with them, and it took us over an hour to break the first one. But she made her biscuits with love, from scratch, with flour, real lard and water. Sometimes she had buttermilk to add to the recipe. She didn't neatly cut them with a cookie cutter or water glass to make them round; they were lumpy with hard top and bottom crusts. They were genuine country cathead biscuits so named because they were about the size of a cat's head.

We kids were not allowed in the round-topped refrigerator. If we needed something, we asked for it. There wasn't much in there, anyway. But I had one important job each morning: getting the butter out for the biscuits.

Mother used stick butter most of the time; other times she'd find big round cakes of it on sale, big bricks that weighed about half a pound. I stood near the refrigerator and awaited her signal, then set the butter on the table next to biscuits so hot you couldn't even touch them.

The little refrigerator was probably built in the Forties. It was small, only head-high to my petite mother. It was nearly silent and kept the food cold. But the small freezer compartment was more interesting to me. It was a bare aluminum box with a door. It was small, only taking up one corner of the top section. She'd have to chip a thick coat of ice off it with a dull butter knife once a month or the frost would fill the entire compartment. She only used it for ice, really; filling aluminum trays that had a set of divided flat plates. You filled the tray with water and dropped in the grid of dividers that would make individual ice cubes. To get a cube, you had to pull up on the handle, and the plates shifted to crack the cubes loose.

Somehow I got it into my mind that the fridge wasn't cold enough. Every time I'd return the butter to the fridge, I'd swing open the freezer door and set the butter on top of the ice trays. Mother would fuss later, saying it was going to take forever to thaw it out.

But I was a stubborn kid, and she didn't seem to appreciate what I was trying to do for her. If the freezer was colder, it should work better at keeping butter fresh. I kept doing it, no matter how many times she fussed.

I went to visit her about five years before she passed. She was happy living on her own in her apartment. We had a great time talking about old times, current events in our lives, my new sweetheart P.J., and what the future would bring.

I got ready to go. It was a five hundred mile trip back home. She'd sipped a lot of coffee as we talked. While she was away in the bathroom, I slipped the butter into the freezer.

17

MOTHER LIED

There was only one time in her short sixty-six years that Mother lied to me. She was a sweet woman who put others before herself; a woman whose code of right and wrong was not relative to the situation--it was absolute and unchanging. She'd been raised in a family so strict that her doctor had to tell her where babies came from. She had been married a year and a half at the time, and was several months pregnant with my oldest sister. But there was one time she fibbed to spare my feelings.

Mother had to leave her job at a muffler shop, where she had worked doing pipe bending and welding, to care for her new infant, Rachael. She spent two weeks in labor at the hospital, resulting in huge hospital bills that they struggled with for years. Rachael was healthy and happy, a cute redheaded child. It took an enormous physical toll on Mother as well. At twenty-five, she'd had her fourth and final child.

I was only four when Rachael arrived home in a laundry basket, but I could tell Mother hurt when she got home from the hospital. For two weeks, she was forced to comply with bed rest orders. She kept us fed, but every time she got out of bed, she left a trail of blood. I would wait until she went back to bed and wrestle the big string mop that weighed more than me, making sure the floor tile floor was clean. Mother cried the first time she caught me doing it. I couldn't do much to help, but I wanted to help her somehow. Mother would get up long enough to prepare Rachael's diapers for washing. The preparation was pretty basic: chug them in the toilet, by hand, and put them into a basket for the washing machine. Disposable diapers were still several years away.

Rachael's arrival coincided with a trucking strike that greatly reduced our family income. We moved into a tarpaper shack in the country as soon as Mother was on her feet, a place we rented from a nice lady, Mrs. Jackson. Things were rough for Mother.

With the truckers on strike and drivers like my Dad limited in their choices of fill-in work, we were barely making it. I was five--old enough to get around but too young for school. With some trepidation, she asked me to go up to the roadside and pick up cigarette butts while she tended the baby. She gave me a can and instructions not to cross the road or get into traffic. I returned with a can half-full. She looked relieved as she peeled the remaining tobacco from the butts to stuff into a corncob pipe. She was a smoker with a monkey on her back, and there hadn't been money for cigarettes for a long time.

We had lived there about a year when I started first grade. I would see laundry hanging on the line through the bus window, and find Mother inside busily ironing clothes. It seemed normal enough, but after a while I noticed that it wasn't just once a week, it was every day. She wore out one wringer washer, and an aunt donated another. One day, I finally asked her, "Mamma, are you taking in washing and ironing?" She looked surprised but told me, "No, honey, I'm just helping Mrs. Satterfield next door. Her washer is broke."

I didn't argue with Mother about taking in the washing. I was skeptical, but it was plausible. As the weeks wore on and I saw that Mrs. Satterfield's machine never got fixed, I knew that Mother was doing everything she could to keep us fed. She wouldn't have accepted government assistance even had it existed back then. But taking in washing and ironing was a tangible line that admitted that you were poor. Very poor. I hoped the other kids on the bus wouldn't notice. Thankfully, none of them ever said anything.

I finally asked her about it fifteen or twenty years later, when we were reliving old times. She stammered and blushed, and admitted that she had lied, and asked me to forgive her. Forgive her?

Mother proved that a moral compass still gives more reliable directions than a moral GPS. I adopted her ethical belief that there is a small core of unacceptable behavior that is absolutely wrong. Perhaps someone should condense it into a Top Ten list and post it where criminals congregate, like at the courthouse. But in this case, she deserves a free pass. Six years after her passing, she is missed; she is loved; she is still making an impact. Mother, you made a difference, and you are still remembered with respect by a lot of people.

18

CRACK KILLS

One summer afternoon when I was five, I hunted down our grandfather. Granny said he was under the house. He was going to level the floor. Even though he rented, he took care of the place like it was his own. Maybe they knocked something off the rent, but I don't know.

The underside of the house was a favorite place to play. There was only two feet of headroom underneath the main house but the front porch was a good four feet off the ground with plenty of light to see. We would take Tonka trucks and Matchbox cars under there and play in the shade. The clay beneath the house had turned to fine dry powder, in places several inches deep. We would look for the little depressions that were the home of "doodle" bugs and use small sticks to stir them to the surface where we examined them. We dug out "roly-poly" bugs, too. We learned a lot about nature from Pawpaw and our uncles--which bugs bit; which ones stung; how to recognize and respond to a non-poisonous black snake. I found Pawpaw far up under the house, just setting up a hydraulic house jack.

"What you doing, Pawpaw?" I asked. "I gotta jack up this beam a couple of inches. The floor is sagging." "Why is it sagging?" I inquired as I scooted closer to see in the dim light. "See those piles of rocks? That's what the house sits on, the foundation that holds it up. That one pile has settled. I have to raise this beam up and re-lay that column."

I sat close by his elbow while he set up. He had a short, thick beam to span the floor joists and a pile of wooden wedges. He got the jack on level ground and slowly jacked it up with one hand as he held the short beam atop it with his other hand.

"What are the wedges for?" I asked. He smiled and pointed at another beam with wedges sticking out. "You get it as close as you can to level and re-lay the rocks, but you don't use too much mortar. You have to use wedges to take up the slack between the top of the rocks and the bottom of the beam."

I was skeptical that wedges could hold up a house without shattering, but if Pawpaw said so, it was true. "Won't the wedges break? How do you keep them from popping out?" I puzzled. "See how there are two of them, one on each side? You tap a little on each one and it raises the floor just a little. Tap a little on one side, tap a little on the other side, and they slide across each other. When they're tight, the weight of the house holds 'em in place. You use hickory wedges. They have to be really strong, really hard." "Oh," I replied.

He had taken up the slack in the jack, and his short support beam met two floor joists over our heads. I watched with great interest. Two more pumps on the jack handle, and a loud 'crack' came from the floor, right above our heads. It sounded like a rifle shot. I cussed. "It's falling!" I blurted out. "Run!" Before my words even echoed off the floor, my feet were paddling, but my feet got little traction in the loose dirt. Instinctively, I tried to run, hitting my head on the floor joists. I cussed on every impact. "Crazy old man! Trying to kill me!" I slid. I scooted. I rolled. Finally, I shot out into the daylight, panting. The cloud of red dust that chased me never caught up. I stood across the driveway waiting for the house to fall. "Pawpaw! Get out of there!" I shouted at the side of the house. All I heard was roaring laughter. "No, it's all right boy!" he shouted back.

Pawpaw emerged a few minutes later. When he did emerge, he was covered in red dust from one end to the other. The dust on his face was streaked with tears. He broke into laughing fits every few minutes until supper, and at odd times for several days afterwards. He thought it was so funny that he intervened when Granny tried to wash my mouth out with soap for my foul language. "Just let that boy be," he chuckled to her, and she knew he meant business.

Pawpaw retold that tale over and over for many years. It was one of the last stories he relived with me before he died. I miss that old man.

19

REFRIGERATOR SURPRISE

Our father would promise to take us fishing, "This weekend." Sometimes he did. It was an exciting adventure. Our favorite fishing spot was on Line Creek in the farm country where Peachtree City has since sprouted. Anyone could slide down the rocks or fish there. The journey was as good as the bream fishing. We would sit in the back of his black 1950 Ford pickup, the wind whipping our hair as we rode out Highway 54. Then we turned onto a dirt road than ran parallel and back the way we had come until it dead-ended at the swimming hole. He would run slow so we could drop the tailgate and drag our feet on the dirt road as we putted along.

As soon as we got a promise of a fishing trip, we set to work collecting bait. We would find a large tin can to hold our prizes. We would spend days looking under leaves and logs for worms. Large night crawlers made the best bait. You could break them into three or four pieces if you ran your hook lengthwise into the body like Dad showed us. At first we kept the cans under our bed, where it was cool and dark. But the worms dried out in two or three days, even with a bit of dirt in the can's bottom. Everything we'd learned about storage advised to keep things in a cool, dry place, or in the refrigerator.

One spring we had an abundance of night crawlers for a fishing trip that was still four days away. We knew they would only last two days, tops, under the bed and they kept escaping. We hit upon a novel idea. They would keep forever in the refrigerator, and wouldn't crawl around as much when they were cold. After supper, we sat all three cans on the bottom ledge of the little fridge.

The next morning, we heard bellows we had never heard before, with a chorus of uncontrolled female laughter. It would be several years before Joe Cocker and his backup singers replicated that sound.

Our worms--lots of worms--had explored the dark recesses of the refrigerator. They were in the butter. They were in the two cold plates of leftovers. They were everywhere, and if anything, the cold had made them more, not less, active.

Dad was mad but Mother intervened once we owned up to our plan, "You *told* them you'd take them fishing, and that's that."

Dad was still mad and didn't take us fishing for a month. We learned to ask Mother if we could store our worms in the fridge, and she provided tin-foil covers for our cans.

She managed to clean and cook the smallest of our trophy bream in a mix of flour and corn meal, fish so small you had to rake their ribs with a fork rather than fillet them.

Those were still the sweetest-tasting fish we ever ate.

20

MISTAKEN IDENTITY

My Dad tinkered with a lot of older cars when I was a kid. He had horse-traded his cousin for a black 1950 Ford pickup that he liked a lot. It had a rounded cab and a bench seat so high my feet didn't reach the floor. It had wide running boards beneath the doors and short running boards in front of the rear fenders. I liked the long tapered door handles with the little flipper that covered the keyhole.

One evening, he drove me the mile or so to our favorite little corner store. They had a dirt parking lot, and we splashed through the big mud hole that lived at the side driveway, parking next to a pine tree near the street corner. He gave me a dollar and instructions to get Mother two packs of cigarettes, a Coke and a peppermint patty. I could keep the change.

I slid down onto the running board and dodged the smaller puddles in the middle of the parking lot. I paid for the items on the list and the clerk handed me back 35 cents. I thought hard about how to spend the rest. I bought two more candy bars and two more peppermint patties.

It had been overcast all day. When I came out of the store, it was dark. Really dark. I avoided all but one small puddle as I circled behind the truck. I pulled down on the long door handle above my head and hauled myself in using the armrest. I sat the paper bag on the seat and chattered excitedly to my Dad about how much stuff I was able to get. During the trucking strike, there had been no money for a 25-cent weekly allowance. He was back at work, and this was the first such treat in a long time.

I was effusive. First, I let him know that I got everything on the list. Then I launched into how much stuff I was able to get with the change, and that everyone would get something, with a nickel to spare.

I got Jake and Doris their favorite candy bars, and I had two peppermint patties I could spread out over a couple of days.

Dad was silent, just staring ahead. When I got no answer, I shifted my attention from the bag I was inventorying and looked up at him. Except it wasn't my Dad. I was confused. The man chuckled and flipped on the overhead light. I looked around the parking lot. Pickup truck taillights glowed from the other side of the parking lot. My face burned. I mumbled, "I'm sorry" and made a hasty exit, careful to close his door without slamming it.

I trotted over to the *other* 1950 Ford pickup and repeated the process of hoisting myself aboard. My Dad fussed over why it took so long, so I pointed at the pickup and just mumbled, "Wrong truck." It was some time before his laughter subsided enough to shift into first gear. Those are ancient trucks now, but they were fifteen years old then, and not all that common. What were the chances of two of them arriving at the same time, and him taking the same spot after my Dad moved across the lot?

Embarrassment is a great thing. It keeps you from getting overconfident. Fear of it keeps you out of trouble. And it provides the best stories to tell the other old folks gathered around the retiree tables at Hardee's.

21

OFF TO SCHOOL

I finally went off to school in the fall of 1967. Since my birthday fell in February, the school wouldn't let me start any sooner. I was itching to join my brother at his school. Mother was occupied with my toddling little sister but she spent lots of time on educational games and taught me to read and write a little. Back then, kindergarten was largely a private school realm, and the expectation was that you'd learn to read and write in first grade. If your parents taught you ahead of time, you had a significant lead.

I'd watched as Doris then Jake started school. I wanted to go too. Sometimes it was boring at home. Finally, outfitted with my rust-colored hooded jacket and a clear yellow umbrella, I got on the bus for the first time.

My parents had eased the little apprehension I had about going to school by telling me I'd have the same teacher that my brother had when he was in first grade, Mrs. Pabst. I'd met her during one of the parent-teacher days. She was nice—a tall pretty brunette with a warm smile.

When I got off the bus, I went straight to Mrs. Pabst's room and found a seat. In the days before backpacks, we used school satchels. Mine was fully armed with big Number One pencils and first-grade writing paper. I even had a couple of my writing samples stuffed in there.

The bell rang, and she called roll. When she'd called the last name her brow furrowed, and she asked me my name. I told her, and she checked her list…twice. She told me to wait and disappeared for a few minutes. When she reappeared, she steered me out the door and into the classroom next door. A chunky white-haired lady smiled when

Mrs. Pabst handed me off to her. I was led to a seat near the back of the room.

We learned ABCs and Mrs. Hall assessed our skills. About half the class could already read and write, at least a little. The class got quiet when she gave us some exercises to do. I headed out the front door, but was intercepted by Mrs. Hall. "I'm supposed to be next door," I explained, my satchel in hand. "No, take your seat and do your work."

The two classrooms shared an adjoining bathroom. This old lady was nice, but she clearly didn't understand. Once I was sure she was busy with paperwork and the kids were intent on their drawing, I quietly slipped my leather satchel from beneath the desk, eased open the wide door, and passed through the bathroom to the class next door. Mrs. Pabst was out of the room and the kids were busy. I took an empty seat and laid out my tools.

It was probably two or three hours before Mrs. Pabst noticed me. She had me gather my stuff and handed me back to Mrs. Hall, "One of yours got away. He was next door." Mrs. Hall didn't ask any questions, but sent me back to my seat.

The next day, I was sure to get a good seat in Mrs. Pabst's classroom right away. I picked a spot right near the middle, where I could see the blackboard better. I'd had trouble seeing from the back of Mrs. Hall's class. This time she didn't notice me when she called roll. I had a good time with the other kids and enjoyed doing the work. The day was half over before Mrs. Hall came in asking if she'd seen me. Once again, they marched me to the seat in the back of Mrs. Hall's class. "But I'm supposed to be in Mrs. Pabst's class," I protested. "No, you are in Mrs. Hall's class, and you have to stay there," Mrs. Pabst explained. My lip stuck out. "But my Mother told me that I'd be in your class, like my brother was." Mrs. Pabst thought for a moment, "Oh, Jake, I remember him. But no, you'll be in Mrs. Hall's class. She is really nice. A great teacher." Clearly they didn't understand.

After a week of sneaking into Mrs. Pabst's class and being ejected, they stuffed a note into my pocket. The next day my Mother took me to school. "He is a good student and gets along fine, but he won't stay in his seat," Mrs. Hall explained. They paused to ask me why. I puffed up. "These teachers sure are dumb. They keep putting me in the wrong class. My Mother told me I'd be in Mrs. Pabst's class, and my Mother don't lie!"

They finally got it. Mrs. Hall called in Mrs. Pabst and all three ladies persuaded me that there wasn't enough room in Mrs. Pabst's class, and that I'd have to stay in Mrs. Hall's class. Once I heard it from my Mother, I accepted the change. I didn't actually mind—Mrs. Hall was nice and treated her kids in a kind, grandmotherly kind of way. She was especially good at teaching the kids to read and making the SRA Reader stories interesting. I can still recall a few of those individual SRA lessons. "Okay, I wanted to do it the way Jake did it. But I like Mrs. Hall," I replied.

There were no further problems. Mrs. Hall laid a firm educational foundation, and even noticed my inability to see the blackboard. Early into the school year, I got my first eyeglasses, and discovered all kinds of things I'd never seen before. Mrs. Hall opened my eyes to many new things. I wish I could express my appreciation to her in person.

22

SOLE SURVIVORS

Each summer we would get a new pair of Keds High-Tops that were expected to last through the year. You could get a pair for a dollar if you shopped around. I had been wearing a pair of Buster Brown leather shoes for a year and a half, and they had split open at the back like sun-ripened possums to accommodate my growing feet. They were even beyond the ability of Brother James, a devout shoemaker in College Park. He preached on Sundays but the rest of the week he fixed shoes. He gave it his awl and he saved a lot of soles. My shoes let water in, and I had to shuffle slowly to keep my feet from slipping out.

It had been a tough year for my parents the year I started first grade. The truck line had been on strike for a year, and my father had to make do with odd jobs. He said that union rules inhibited him from taking a competing driving job during the strike. We had to move from the apartment to a tarpaper shack with an outhouse and a well way out in the yard. He borrowed an old dump truck from his cousin and made survival wages cleaning out old houses as hippies vacated them. He took on an armed security officer's job, and we greeted him with cheery anticipation each evening, "Did you shoot anyone *today*?" We subsisted on nothing but biscuits and gravy for months. I still can't stand gravy.

I was determined to take great care of my new Keds. They would have to last me a year—maybe more—and my father had said that if I didn't take care of them, I wouldn't get another pair. I lined them up carefully under my bed. Not good enough. I tried putting them into the dresser drawer that my mother had used as my bed when I was a baby, but the bottom was coming loose--still no good. I didn't want to just leave them out in the open. We had rats that probably had a taste for new shoes.

I fretted over the shoes long after everyone else went to bed. I finally hit upon the perfect place, a bastion no rat could enter. A place surrounded by cast iron, the safest place in the house.

The wood stove had a side door just big enough for a small biscuit pan, and I would be up before Mother awoke. I could show her my clever hiding place first thing. I brushed out the oven compartment and lined up the two shoes neatly inside. I went to bed, my mind finally at rest.

I awoke to a loud, metallic clank-clank and the smell of burning kindling. I flew from the bed, yelling at my mother, "My shoes are in the stove!" She just stared back, since the statement didn't really make sense to anyone else, nor should it. By the time I explained it two more times, thick black smoke was rolling across the ceiling.

I was even madder than my parents, and for months I accused her of deliberately baking those shoes. After all, how could anyone not check the stove for shoes and other loose gear before lighting it up? I grumpily put the worn-out Buster Browns on and went to school. It was spring before the Keds were replaced. We ate Keds-flavored biscuits for weeks afterward, which didn't add to my own popularity.

I was 35 the last time I saw that little wood stove squatting on three legs beneath a massive black walnut behind my uncle's house. I opened the oven door and marveled at how small the soles were, still attached to the stove. Truly sole survivors.

23

THINKING INSIDE THE BOX

Christmas was an exciting time for my siblings and me, but it wasn't just about the stuff. Some years we only got nuts in our stockings and crates of apples and oranges. It was usually too cold to play outside much, so it was easy to get caught up in the music and smiles of others.

Christmas 1967 was different. The previous Christmas had been the coldest on record. Temperatures of eight below zero had tempered the fun of playing in the snow. I had gotten a touch of frostbite playing in the snow, but nothing serious. This year it was warm and the trucking strike had ended after eighteen months, just in time for Christmas.

We waited up for Santa for what seemed like an eternity in our young concept of passing time. We awoke as daylight was just breaking. We hit the floor running. The stockings were bulging, and we went for the nuts first. I liked the thin-shelled walnuts, and always tackled the Brazil nuts from the mix last, with a hammer. We looked over the flats of apples and oranges. They smelled delicious.

A tree had appeared during the night. The shiny aluminum branches gleamed from the light of the bare incandescent bulb overhead and the low light streaming through the living room window. This year, there were presents under the tree. Quite a few. Our excavations revealed plastic Army men—always a favorite. Jake got two steel Tonka toys—a dump truck and a bulldozer. Doris got dolls and girly things. I got a plastic bear that growled and ran around in random directions. It reversed direction when you shot it with suction cup tipped darts. I had admired it in a store catalogue some weeks before.

We played with the toys for a while. Mother made hot chocolate from scratch, mixing the cocoa powder, sugar and milk. It was scalding hot. She made us a hot breakfast of sausage, eggs, and hard-crust biscuits. Dad chose streak-o-lean bacon. The house swelled from the smells and the sounds of squealing kids.

For a while, there had been no money for the power bill. We'd had to do our homework under the light of kerosene lamps and use Pawpaw's oak icebox for a few months. It worked well enough, but we had to drive five miles to get blocks of ice twice a week. They sold it at the same place we bought coal for the stove. Looking back, I guess our Christmas wasn't that different than one a century earlier.

With the strike over, the lights were on. Dad had even bought an electric pump for the well at the far side of the yard. No more cranking up one bucket at a time using the windlass and carrying the heavy buckets to the house.

Best of all, Mother got a new gas stove. It was small and simple, but it was new. We retired the little wood stove that still smelled of burnt tennis shoes. The box the stove came in was taller than me, and wide. It was sturdy, with reinforced sides. We had never seen a box that large. It took two of us to drag it to the short drop-off between the well and the outhouse at the side of the yard. That side of the yard had fewer of the pine saplings that encroached on the yard.

At first, we tried sliding down the slope. No good. The doubled box was just too stiff. It suddenly stopped, and Jake kept going forward, rolling down the low rise. We studied it for a while, and decided to make a "tank" out of it. One of us would stand inside it, then lean against the inside to tip it over. It was dizzying, but fun. We played in the box until we were damp with December sweat.

We finally got up the nerve to drive our tank down the slope. I went first. We carefully set the box on the precipice of the four-foot gentle slope. When I leaned into it, the box hesitated a second, then dropped over the edge. I couldn't keep my footing on the slippery cardboard, and fell sideways. The box kept rolling until it reached the flat ground at the bottom, rocking to a gentle rest. We took turns, with one inside and their accomplice giving the push necessary to tip it over the edge. We enjoyed this all afternoon--actually, for about a week afterward. Eventually, the staples pulled loose. We used pliers to remove the loose staples and tried using the flat cardboard as a sled, but it just stuck to the ground.

The simplest pleasures are surely the sweetest ones. And it is true that a kid will have more fun with the box than the toy that came in it.

24

PROGRESS

My grandparents grew up in rural Alabama, in an area so remote that even rural electric was slow in coming. Granny was convinced until the day she died that the light bulb had been invented in 1950, because that's when her community got power. It was one of few examples that I can truly call "progress."

Progress can be measured in so many ways that I'm unsure what the term even means, if anything. On a train, it's forward motion, with or without a destination in mind. Don't lemmings make progress toward their own destination? Is it speed—if those lemmings get there faster, are they making better progress? Perhaps it's making something better—but for whom? "Progress" is the main reason cited by developers and city planners to tear down and pave over things. Is it a synonym for destruction? Paving miles of farmland so people can move to "the country," where they still build their houses thirty feet from their neighbors? It's the same as living downtown, except you have a longer commute.

Simply speeding up communications, transportation and the pace of our lives doesn't seem like progress. If it were progress, our time saving devices and techniques would provide us more free time than our ancestors had a generation or two ago. We've made things physically easier and compensated by spending money on gym memberships to prevent our lack of activity killing us.

We could learn to fix things on the car and around the house. We'd get some exercise, save a ton of money, and learn skills along the way that would be useful to ourselves and to our neighbors. If I pay someone to cut my grass then pay to go to a gym, I've paid twice for exercise that should have been free. It amuses me to watch the jockeying for the closest parking spot to the local gym's front door, and how cars have to dodge all the other cars in the gym's fire lane dropping off and picking up twenty-something athletes. A walk across the parking lot is somehow a bad thing when you are there to exercise.

My grandparents understood thrift and that progress requires ever-increasing resources. They had survived the First Depression and understood that fortunes come and go. There might not be as much money available tomorrow as today. They continued many of their country activities even after moving to Georgia's suburbs, both because of thrift and because traditional ways were healthy and effective. The well on the back porch had clean cold water and plenty of it. Sometimes we used a gourd dipper, but the solid tin dipper gave the water a sweeter taste. Granny's old house had no electrified air conditioning, but it had rectangular holes in the perimeter of the floor that drew in cool air from beneath the house. The holes were also good places to sweep the sand she scattered before she swept, and for the mop water to drain. When cold weather came, she dropped wedges into the holes. She'd lower the top sashes of the eight-foot windows to let hot air escape during the day, and at night she would close the top sashes and raise the bottom sashes to let in the cool breeze. It was relatively comfortable and cost nothing to operate and maintain.

Pawpaw and Granny spent very little on food. Corn was preserved in a pit dug into the ground and lined with pine straw. Potatoes would keep for months inside a mound of sandy earth covered by sheets of roofing tin. Granny stretched screen wire across the roof edge, placed her slices of apples, pears and other fruit on it, and weighed down a second layer of screen with rocks to keep the birds off while it dried. The dried fruit was tasty and lasted a long time. You passed between two wreaths of hot peppers to enter the front door. It was a handy place to store them, they kept out bad spirits, and they kept bugs from hovering near the door. She had a big canning shed filled with the tomatoes, pickles and other garden bounty that wouldn't last any other way. A grocery run fit into one or two paper sacks: coffee, flour, sugar, tea, and some bacon and sausage. They didn't have to pay premium prices for organic, and got the extra benefit of physical activity tending the garden.

They spent no money on an exterminator or termite contract. Fly tape curled at each outside door and in the kitchen. Pawpaw used a hand-cranked blower to spread lime across the dirt under the house to discourage insects and rodents from taking up residence. It worked.

PJ and I use as many of their old ways as we can, but I don't miss the outhouse in full summer bloom. It stank like nothing else and attracted flies. Spider bites to one's tender parts while sitting in the outhouse killed quite a few men in the old days. Outhouses attracted rats, which attracted snakes. Granny's outhouse on the forty-acre farm was guarded by a very large Black Racer who disliked trespassers. The old folks taught the kids how to tell the difference between a poisonous moccasin and a harmless black snake, and about the behavior of each. The black racer that lived behind the privy was eight to ten feet long, with a narrow head indicating that he was not poisonous. Pawpaw showed us that although a black racer will chase you, it runs the other way if you turn around and chase after it. It was scary at first, but then the snake was just annoying. Sometimes I'd have to turn around and give chase two or three times to make it back to the house.

So what is the meaning of "progress"? For me it means electricity and indoor plumbing. It's certainly not fast and cheap, the two things my father cautioned me about when I came of dating age. My car was cutting edge when Studebaker built it in 1951, and it still runs well. It was rated at 29 miles per gallon when they still measured it on a test track with wind resistance. That probably translates to 33 miles per gallon the way it's measured on a treadmill inside a building today. Of course it cost more than a Ford in 1951. The most valuable and useful things are elegantly simple and are hard to improve upon. They are durable. Fast, cheap and disposable are the causes and products of fallacy.

25

THE HUT

Pawpaw and Granny bought a large camping tent when I was four or five years old, the kind made of heavy rubberized canvass. It was tall, with heavy flaps you could lower over the doors and windows, and it could easily sleep eight adults. They let my uncles, Dave and Bert, use it and they would keep it set up in a stand of pines about thirty yards behind the outhouse during the warm weather months. The tent was heavy, but apparently very durable: I saw it set up in my Uncle Dave's yard just a few years ago. That tent was a gathering place in my formative years, and a temple of learning.

At the beginning of my seventh summer Pawpaw and Granny took the tent to the Smoky Mountains, leaving us without a fortress. Bert built a crude tree house, but it was cramped, and those of us under four feet tall had trouble climbing up.

Uncle Dave was about sixteen by then, and spent much of his time fixing cars and motorcycles to run the roads. Uncle Bert was only five years older than me, and he spent a lot of time with us. My brother Jake was eight then, and my sister Doris was eleven. Bert had a few casual friends who would wander in and out. But then a new kid moved into Heatherwood, the subdivision still under construction next to Pawpaw's farm, who was different.

For one thing, Junior's family was from up North somewhere. He also had a Polish name that took me a full year to master. He was a fun guy, always in a cheerful mood and ready for any challenge or dare. Sometimes he would dare himself to do things when no one else would dare him. He agreed that the tree house was cramped, and said he could help.

The next time we saw him, he had dragged huge sections of carpet through the woods, laying it out where four pines grew close together on high, sandy ground. He gave vague answers about its origin, at first saying his parents had been away for a long weekend, then saying they had replaced all their carpet and had given it to him. I still don't know if he had permission to cut that carpet out of their house. We were just grateful to have it. He and Bert built a frame between the trees then nailed angled rafters to the trees so our new carpet "Hut" would shed rain properly. It did. We trenched around it to channel water downhill in a hard rain. I don't recall it ever leaking, or even smelling bad (for a carpet tent).

Junior was about twelve that summer. The five of us would roast weenies and marshmallows on the campfire and tell spooky stories, and have lively discussions about how the world worked and who would grow up to be what. We would "ride" saplings to the ground, leaping onto them and springing to the opposite side, careful to let go at just the right moment. We explored the swamp edges, but dared not wade into the dark water. The edges of Atlanta still had quite a few swamps in the Sixties. We saw them filled in one by one as we grew up, with some of them taking years to fill in. They were neat to explore, and had history. During the siege of Atlanta, the swamps around Jonesboro and Riverdale had formed part of a defensive perimeter that kept the Yankees out. Some Atlantans argue for digging them out again, the same people who clamor to outlaw air conditioning.

Bert taught us how to build rabbit traps out of scrap lumber. He would make a long skinny box with a door that slid up and a trigger at the back that dropped the door behind the rabbit. We learned together how to retrieve the rabbits, and learned the hard way that you needed to stand back and throw rocks at a sprung trap to be sure you had indeed trapped a rabbit. A skunk might await the impatient.

We had no horses, but we played Cowboys and Indians, and traveled the roads with our wagons, collecting the two-cent bounty on Coke bottles to buy penny candy and five-cent cigars. I never finished one. I guess it made us feel grown. Grown people must have spent a lot of time green with nausea. Together, we collected corncobs and swamp reeds and whittled our own corncob pipes. We would collect enough long gray streamers of wild "rabbit tobacco" to fill a pipe and light it. It was dry and harsh, and I never developed a taste for it. Bert tried to teach us how to carve neatly spaced holes into swamp reeds to make flutes and whistles, but we lacked his carving skill.

But sometimes the scant age difference mattered, and we younger kids would be shut out. Bert and Junior built a higher, more elaborate tree house to further exclude the smaller kids. It was a well built house about four times my own four-foot height off the ground. The rungs were too far apart for the smaller kids to easily climb. It had a central room hugging the tree, and a railed porch that went all the way around. When Junior got a pellet rifle, he and Bert holed up in the tree house to target practice and shoot at birds.

One day, Jake, Doris and I were roasting weenies on the fire by the Hut, griping about the older boys hogging the pellet gun. We were bored and miffed that they had shut us out. We shouted back and forth to them in the tree house but they just taunted us. Suddenly we heard a crash, and I looked just in time to see the tree house roof hit the ground and fly in all directions. Unfortunately, the porch that held Bert and Junior had been under that roof. The whole affair had collapsed straight down, all at once, falling twelve to fifteen feet. Somehow Bert and Junior were thrown off as it hit the ground, rolling away from the tree.

The shock lasted only a millisecond before we let loose howls of laughter and taunts at them. I took an early lead in running, since my shorter legs gave me a known disadvantage. Bert and Junior eventually caught up to us all, and we each received a pummeling for laughing at them. It was a great summer to be a kid.

26

JUNIOR IS TRANSFORMED

Junior was a major participant in our activities and was like one of the family. He would hang out and eat at Pawpaw's and watch Bonanza on the old black and white console TV about twice a week on a not-to-interfere-with-TV-wrestling basis. I guess he watched too many episodes.

On a particularly slow day, when nothing was moving—not the wind, not our retired bloodhound Duke, not even the July Flies (cicadas) Junior suddenly arose from his blanket. "I'm going home. I bet I can stomp the fire out, just like on TV." Even though we cleared the underbrush and pine needles away from our camp, we always went to great lengths to ensure the campfire was cold before leaving camp.

"Just dare me to do it." We looked up at him with furrowed brows, but no one took up his challenge. The fire had died down, but there was a good bed of pine embers on the sandy soil that would need to be watered down, then covered with sand. We worried about brush fires even though Pawpaw had the fire department help him burn off the underbrush every two years to keep down the ticks and spiders. Although the patch of woods around the camp covered at least twenty acres, you could see almost to the edge of it through the tree trunks.

"You shouldn't" drifted up lazily at the same time another sniped, "You can't." That was all the provocation Junior needed. He jumped, landing in the center of the shallow fire pit on his brand-new Keds and he began furiously stomping the ground beneath. He said he was putting out the fire "cowboy style," although his stooped stomping made him look more like a TV Indian. We rolled back to avoid the sparks, but those flew straight up anyway.

He stomped out most of the fire before he cried out, "Ahhh! Ahhh!" First he tried to pat out the flames clinging to the cloth of his

Keds; then he tried stomping harder, in circles. Now he did look like a caricature of an Indian doing who knows what kind of dance (rain, to douse his feet?) and our skeptical disinterest turned to paralyzing laughter.

He suddenly rose to his full lanky height, standing straight as Bonanza's Adam Cartwright.

Pandemonium broke out. We could see that the rubber edges of his Keds were alight, and rapid-fire shouts rang out. "Take your shoes off!" "Pour water on them!" "Sit down!"

Junior heeded none of our advice. He made two laps around the campfire and lit off down the sandy path toward home, his screams fading away. Our stomachs hurt. We were immobilized by laughter and had spent our breath tossing him those few words of advice. We sure didn't have the wind to chase after him, pull him to the ground, and remove his offending shoes.

It was several minutes before we recovered enough to check on him. We had heard his repeated cries of "Ahhh!" "My feet are on fire!" get fainter as he had run off into the woods. We were uncertain which path he had taken.

We walked, still unable to run, along the main path leading from the hut. There were actually several paths crossing the wood, but his track was easy to follow. The smell of burning rubber was pungent, and about every ten or twenty feet we found a flaming bit of rubber sole. His strides had been really long ones. He must have looked like Mercury as he streaked through the pine forest on his blazing feet.

Bert ran on to Junior's house, where he found him with his feet immersed in a pan of water, complaining that we had laughed at him. The rest of us had hung back to put out several small pine needle fires before they could spread, and we covered the bits of burning rubber before going home.

Junior had run the soles completely out of the shoes, arriving home with only the smoldering canvas sides on his blistered feet. He stayed home for a week while they healed.

I don't normally laugh at the pain of others, even when the cause is their own stupidity. But that story is sure to resurface at every family reunion, and those of us who witnessed Junior's transformation into a god are still incapacitated with laughter.

27

GROWN-UP PURSUITS

We didn't grow up too soon from our pursuit of grown-up activities. That occurred because we had to go to work at eleven or twelve to keep food on the table. We did apply our curiosity to enough adult activities to persuade us to enjoy being a kid. Sneaking a wide-eyed peek at a pilfered Playboy or smoking a fourth of a nasty cigar was still fun (it still is sometimes).

The summer of 1968 was unbearably hot and dry--enough to keep us closer to the house. As we hovered like tired flies around the back porch well, we watched Pawpaw cut up a bushel of peaches into an old churn. When he said he was making wine, we were filled with questions. He added some sugar, some yeast, and I'm not sure what else to the mix before he covered it with cheesecloth. "Now, ya'll stay out of that, it's for grown-ups."

We were skeptical that anyone could make their own wine. Pawpaw had only taken cold well water and dumped some stuff in it—we knew only Jesus could turn water into wine, or maybe those people from Martini and Rossi on TV. Pawpaw seemed capable of doing or learning anything, but we had never seen him make wine before. "How long does it take?" Doris asked. "About six weeks, if you leave it alone. If the weather is warm enough, you can make two batches." He sat the churn on the workbench of his garden shed, up behind the dog pen that held Duke, a retired Redbone Hound tracking dog the sheriff had given him.

Duke was friendly, but big, and we were just a little afraid of him. We waited until we were sure Duke was asleep when we checked on the wine every week. It developed funny smells, and a skin formed on the surface. We were there when Pawpaw skimmed the fruit from the mixture, gently mixing the liquid again.

By the fourth week, it was too hot to go out and play at all. There had been no cooling rain all summer, and the house only had one fan that pulled air from the back porch window through the house and out the front porch window. It was the year that Pawpaw set fire to a five-foot tree stump in the yard, and without rain, it burned day and night for two months.

"He's going to bottle it in two weeks," my sister said as we stood around the churn. "You think it's ready enough yet?" I asked. It smelled like wine—the over-ripe peach smell had been replaced with a sharp, tangy smell. "He'll catch us," Jake chimed in. "Not if we only take a little of it. Let's give it a taste," I offered.

We had brought a well dipper with us, the kind made of solid tin that gave well water a sweet taste. We each took a turn, and it didn't taste too bad. Maybe an 'electric' sensation on the back of the tongue, but sweet and just peachy. We only filled the dipper half full, passing it around twice. We agreed that it wasn't too bad, but that it wasn't finished yet.

The rebellion began about two hours later. All three of us were burping up fermented peaches. Cramps doubled us over, and when the cramps ebbed, herds of antelope took their afternoon stroll through our bowels on hoofs just sharpened at the nail salon. Then our middle became the center of explosions radiating out in two directions. We were ill. Doris, being oldest and biggest, won the battle for the outhouse door. Jake, bigger than me, seized the one bathroom in the house trailer we lived in at the back of the farm. I made a beeline for a chamber pot in Granny's house.

Granny was irritated at the interruption, demanding, "Go use the outhouse!" "But Doris is in there," I cried, holding my stomach. "Then go home and use the toilet." "Jake is on that one," I whined. Now she knew we'd been up to something, and Granny was good at prying details from anyone. Especially from kids—it was how she collected her gossip. I spilled everything, including the details of our nefarious plan.

Pawpaw gathered us all together once we could stand, and asked us directly if we had gotten into his wine. We readily admitted it. "Did you learn something from it?" "We sure did, Pawpaw, I never been that sick," Jake groaned. "Go on home, then," he chuckled. Pawpaw was a great teacher of life lessons. He gave you room to run, and if you got a bump or bruise from some ill conceived or clumsily executed action, he'd ask you, "What did you learn from that?" I seldom made the same mistake twice.

Except that we did exactly the same thing when he brewed beer the next spring. Then we were fully convinced.

28

WE GET RELIGION

Brother Lee's church sat almost on the worn edge of the playground of my second grade school. It was a low white building that was Adams' Grocery before the old man retired. Every Saturday, we endured an Octagon soap bath in the Number Three galvanized washtub to be ready for God on Sunday. Mother would heat the water on the wood stove and we'd take turns bathing in the same tub of lukewarm water. My Granny pronounced it "oxygen" soap and she liked it because it was the closest substitute to the lye soap she made in her outdoor cauldron back in Alabama. It was strong enough to remove dirt, skin, and minor sins.

Sundays, our parents dressed me and my brother Jake in our little suits: his in blue, mine in green. Doris had a girly dress appropriate to representing the family to the Lord, or at least to the congregation. Granny had bought us those suits for Easter the previous year, and they were nice.

Brother Lee was a down to earth minister, the kind who held an outside job and preached on Sunday. He asked for no material support from our little church, just our spiritual support. He gave thought-provoking sermons, building from a slow plowman's walk to a marching cadence to a full trot like a coon dog on a fresh scent. What I remember best about him was his sincerity and passion.

I didn't mind listening to him preach, but kids can get fidgety, especially on a late Spring morning when it's too warm for a suit jacket that you aren't allowed to remove. As we listened to Brother Lee's wind-up, we looked around at the other members until Granny silently twisted my ear half off. We moved back a row and shifted around in our seats, looking out at the willow limbs swaying back and forth in the bright sun. The windows were flung wide, and the big cargo door behind the pulpit stood wide open to keep the fiery preacher cool. We slid around quietly on the pew and fingered through the hymnals. We read both sides of every colorful fan in the book tray in front of us. There were a few mixed in from used car lots and other businesses, but most were given to churches by the local funeral homes. The trussed-up ladies made liberal use of the cardboard and stick fans.

After the third song, *Will the Circle be Unbroken*, we took advantage of everyone standing to ease out the front door. We ducked a couple of carpenter bees as we walked around the cars and studied how oddly soft the mossy ground felt under our leather Sunday shoes. I wondered aloud whether the soft ground covered unmarked graves in the dirt parking lot, but Jake didn't think so. We walked down the side of the church to the back, right behind the preacher. The floor was just the right height to stand comfortably, resting our chins and arms on the cargo door threshold. We were still interested in how to treat our fellow man and act honestly, and we listened attentively.

As he shifted into third gear, Brother Lee let out a whoop and pointed at the sky, nearly leaping out of his penny loafers. He continued a little longer, and when he suddenly kicked his foot backward as he slammed the pulpit, his shoe went flying and grazed the side of my head. Before I could react, he jumped into the air and flung the other shoe just over Jake's scalp.

It was pure reflex, and we didn't mean to do it. We both let out a profanity that echoed against the front door of the church. We ducked down, awaiting a lightning strike, or at least the arm of the preacher dragging us up through the cargo door. We got neither. A thick silence hung in the air like a punted football until it was broken by sidesplitting laughter. The youngest didn't laugh--they just stared wide-eyed at us. But the parents and old folks held their bellies and laughed. Brother Lee turned and cracked a smile at us, then he laughed aloud too before he turned back to his sermon.

Still, we wandered the churchyard for another twenty minutes before we dared set foot in God's house. We slipped in even more quietly than we had eased out, and took seats near the door.

Oddly, we were never even chastised for the outburst. I guess they understood it was accidental and they had seen the horror on our faces. Pawpaw, an old mule-driving farmer himself, ribbed Brother Lee about needing a blacksmith around if he continued to throw shoes. We learned not to stand behind a shoe-throwing preacher ever again.

29

FAKED OUT

Uncle Dave and Uncle Bert liked to pull practical jokes on us, on each other; on just about anybody. Among Dave's teenaged favorites was the fake dog poop he had purchased from the back of a comic book along with the X-ray Specs that left me cross-eyed for days.

Early on, it was funny to see Granny throw a hissy fit when she saw the pile next to the bed of Pixie, her snake-killing Spaniel. Dave was good at leaving it next to a doorframe, where you only caught it out of the corner of your eye.

We knew Dave would be out all day one July Saturday, and Granny and Pawpaw were off somewhere all weekend. Bert initiated the prank, but I eagerly joined in with Doris and Jake to pull it off properly.

Bert found some of Pixie's poop and scraped it up onto some cardboard. We took it back to Granny's house and laid a layer of newspaper across the entire table. We laid the rubber poop on the newspaper, and used Popsicle sticks and small branches to swirl the real poop on the cardboard sheet into the exact shape and size as Dave's rubber poop. When we noticed the color and consistency was off a bit, Bert sent us out to find some mud and more poop of the correct hue. It took an hour and a half of collecting and a half-hour of mixing to make a perfect replica.

We left it on Granny's favorite farmhouse table, her favorite because Jim Nabors used to eat at that table when they were neighbors in Sylacauga. Beside the cardboard, we left a white sheet of paper that said only, "Surprise!"

About four o'clock, Dave came home. The dining room was in the middle of the house, on the path between the back porch and the front porch. The back door was the primary entrance, since it adjoined the well and the kitchen. We waited quietly on the front porch. We knew we wouldn't keep a straight face if we actually saw him, and we wanted an easy escape route.

We listened intently. Dave opened the Frigidaire and poured himself some sweet tea, then we heard him crunch, then blow his breath in and out. Granny kept both sweet onions and hot onions, and we'd often grab an onion to eat. The hot ones would bring tears and take your breath away.

We heard Dave's footsteps head from the kitchen toward the living room that faced the front porch. We sat still until we heard him chuckle, "That ain't real!" and heard a hand slap the table. We were halfway off the porch by the time his first sentence of profanity reached us. No matter how sweetly he called, none of us would approach within 20 feet of him for days.

A few days later, Bert's friends were over. His friend John was loud and overconfident but not real bright. Still a pretty good kid, though. We relived last night's episode of Laugh-In before we fell into a bored silence. Bert looked at the paper towel roll in the middle of the table. Paper towels were a new invention then.

"Hey, John, you seen that White Tornado commercial where it sucks up the water?" "Yeah, Bounty." "I'll bet you fifty cents that I can make it work." "No way, that's just TV." Bert poured a few ounces of water beneath the table. "They'd get sued if it didn't work—I'll bet ya. I'll give you fifty cents if it don't work." Bert pretended to try it for two or three minutes and crawled back out, puzzled. "I guess I'm not doing it right, but it worked on the commercial." We all had seen the commercial. The towel created a tornado that sucked the water right off a counter, off a table, and even off a floor. The White Tornado was on frequently from the time TV programming started at six in the morning until the national anthem and test pattern announced the end of daily programming at midnight.

A skeptical John crawled under the high wooden table. We leaned over to check his progress. "This ain't working." "You have to hold it *just above* the water—now you're too high." John's hand got tired, and he dunked the towel into the water. "No, now you're too low. It sucks it up like a vacuum cleaner—you can't actually *touch* the water with it." "It'll work, but you have to concentrate."

John's brow furrowed, his determination deepening. Now he felt obliged to prove that it would work. He didn't want to fail, and he wanted to show up Bert. "Okay, okay, you gotta be quiet. I gotta concentrate." "I saw a little go up onto it!" I teased.

Fifteen minutes into the effort, the giggles started, quiet at first, with one person's snickers setting off the next like kindling alight. John got really stiff. His upper lip rose, taking his nose with it, and his nostrils flared.

A red-faced John slid stiffly from beneath the table. Bert gave John two quarters, real silver ones, and tearfully told him it was worth every penny. We scattered and regrouped at the Hut to tell and retell the story.

I guess we all lose innocence a bit at a time. It just seems that we had a lot more of it to lose growing up back then.

30

RING OF FIRE

We didn't watch much TV growing up, but we listened to records. Granny watched a TV preacher on Sundays. Pawpaw watched his "rasslin'" on Saturdays, from beautiful downtown Porterdale, a tiny Georgia cotton mill town that was somehow the epicenter of the wrestling circuit for decades. He was a true believer in such characters as Gorgeous George and would fight along with them from his recliner. Once, he flipped over in his recliner, cussing and fighting, with Brother Lee eating dinner in the next room. Pawpaw tumbled backwards out the front door and onto the porch but managed to keep his eyes fixed on the action the whole time. Those referees couldn't be trusted to watch for foul play on their own.

Granny did watch "her stories," which included a couple of soap operas and *Dark Shadows*, the earliest ongoing vampire drama. We kids listened to the radio and to 45 records on a portable record player. Sometimes Bert and Dave took the songs too much to heart. Bert once ran up a big phone bill after listening to Chuck Berry's *Promised Land*. He called every area code he could think of to reach the number "Tidewater four-ten-oh-nine" mentioned in the song. Then he got fascinated with Johnny Cash's song *Ring of Fire*, which was about Cash's battle with drug addiction, though we were too young to understand the reference. Bert sang along until he could do a pretty decent Johnny Cash impression.

He and Dave had been listening to the song for about two months, seemingly non-stop. One morning Bert, Dave, Jake and I stood around kicking dust on the oval go-kart track and chewing on our plug tobacco. Bert broke into a few bars of *Ring of Fire* and we speculated that no one could actually survive being in a ring of fire. We bantered back and forth until Bert went back to the house, returning with a metal gas can. "I'll show you that you <u>can</u> stand in a ring of fire," Bert said. We thought it was foolish and were too squeamish to help him do it, so Bert poured a ring of gasoline onto the bare ground and stood inside it. The circle was only five or six feet across. "Now watch," he said. He dropped a wooden match onto it, but the ring had gaps in it. The fire ran a few feet around the circle and stopped suddenly.

"You ain't doing it right," interjected Dave. He took the can and poured a wider stream, making sure he'd left no gaps. When Bert tossed a match this time, the gasoline lit before the match hit the ground, making a 'whoosh.' "See, told ya," Bert sneered, and he broke into a bar of the song. But the flames didn't die down this time. And they'd poured the fuel in too small a circle. Bert was getting singed. We tried scooping sand onto it, but there wasn't enough sand to make a difference. Bert's eyes widened, and he leapt through the flames once they dropped from head-high to waist-high. His clothes didn't catch fire, but he smelled of burnt hair.

Songs can inspire either good or bad behavior, even outright stupid and potentially lethal actions. Bert learned the hard way that a song is just a song.

31

MIKE'S BAPTISM

Brother Lee was a traditional Baptist minister. Late one May, he announced that the church would have an old-fashioned baptism on the river the following week. To our surprise, among those who stood when the preacher asked who was ready to be baptized was Mike, my second cousin, twice (forcibly) removed. Mike had never been in serious trouble, but he was hardheaded, even with adults, and would go out of his way to do everything he was told not to do. He was quick and sinewy, and he liked to show off to prove himself. He repeatedly proved that he was strong as a rock (and twice as smart). Besides being loud and argumentative, he had a mouth that would make a Navy Master Chief blush.

We all drove down to the low bank of the muddy river armed with Polaroid cameras to capture the memories. My parents piled all four kids into the pink '55 Chevy with a picnic lunch. I took a place in line behind two middle-aged ladies in long modest dresses. The crowd sang *Shall We Gather at the River* before the real work began.

The preacher stood chest deep in the river, too far out to clearly hear his words to those about to go under. He said a few words to them, then tilted them backward and down into the water. He said a few more words while the river washed over them before he tilted them back up again. The ladies beamed as they made their way barefoot to family members waiting with blankets and dry clothes.

I was third in line. I laid my shoes and socks carefully aside and waded in. I wasn't too nervous, despite not being able to swim. I trusted Brother Lee. The river was about 75 feet wide, but shallow. At least the preacher had found a sandbar for the festivities. Brother Lee had to wade closer to shore to match my four-foot height.

Brother Lee asked, "Do you believe?" and when I said, "Yes," he said, "Bend your knees," and under I went, eyes closed against the muddy water. Five seconds, ten seconds, then I was pushed up toward the sunlight and gasped a big breath. He patted my back and I trudged toward shore in my heavy clothes.

An older man went, then two more ladies, then several teenaged girls. Mike was up. We were morbidly curious about Mike being baptized. He wasn't much of a churchgoer, and we made bets on whether he would do it.

Mike peeled off his shoes and socks and waded rather gingerly into the tepid water. He was lanky, and stood nearly as tall as the preacher who had waited for years to baptize Mike. Mike's bevy of sisters cheered him on from beneath a cottonwood tree. We heard the preacher speak to Mike, who took a position to one side of the preacher. Brother Lee shifted positions to catch Mike, and we saw Mike nod just as the preacher leaned him way back. It didn't look like Mike bent his knees, and he'd arched his back.

Mike's hand stuck up from the water like the Lady of the Lake without Excalibur. Brother Lee lifted him up quickly, and Mike sputtered and gasped. He gave the preacher a dirty look and wiped out his eyes. Brother Lee made a somewhat longer speech, but the only word we could distinguish was "sinner." Mike went under again, but it looked like Brother Lee was pushing his chest down instead of supporting his back. The preacher launched into a sermon about saving the worst of the sinners, and went on for quite some time. The preacher had one arm raised to the sky, the other immersed in the muddy river. There was a swirl next to the preacher that the river didn't make, like a big bass taking the bait. Mike's leg broke the surface this time. Mike burst forth, throwing droplets of water far and wide. He scowled at the preacher and whatever Mike said to him was in an irritated tone.

The preacher nodded and rested his hand on Mike's shoulder. He moved Mike out into deeper water to ensure that he would remain covered this time. We giggled. Mike went down for the third time.

Brother Lee got loud this time, going on for a full minute. Mike tried to rise, but Brother Lee held him firmly beneath the water. Some began to count. Others looked at their watches. Five minutes past noon. Seven minutes after. It was a long, long time before Brother Lee looked startled and reached down to raise up Mike with both hands.

We still don't know if he was startled because he'd forgotten Mike, or if Mike bit his leg.

Mike shook his hair like a dog, and scooped his hand into the river to splash water at the preacher. Mike cussed, "Are you stupid, or are you *trying* to kill me?" "You ignorant s********!" "Trying to drown me! I *knew* he didn't like me!" All the while, Mike was stripping off his wet clothes.

In trying to stomp his feet on the river bottom, Mike hit a slick spot, and went down face-first. He got madder each time he slipped and fell, his colorful language adding additional hues to an already colorful spring afternoon. He finally gained the shore near his sisters, whose titters had triggered a rumble of laughter that spread through the crowd like waves from a pebble. Several people laughed so hard they had to step behind cars to relieve themselves.

We never saw Mike at church again.

32

A FINE BORDELLEAUX

Adams had moved out of his house adjacent to his store when he retired from the grocery business. The Craftsman house that was sandwiched between the church and the playground of my elementary school sat vacant for a while, until the ladies moved in.

We didn't see them during church services. But we saw them at recess and we would wander to the edge of the playground. Six or eight college-aged ladies would hang out and smoke on the back porch and talk, and scurry back inside when one of the frequent cars pulled into the front driveway. I didn't know women *had* that much skin—it was normally covered up. I thought it was peculiar that they sat around during the day in their nightclothes. Maybe they worked at night and slept during the day, as my Dad sometimes did at the trucking outfit.

When the teachers caught us looking, they sent dirty looks over to the house. Eventually, one of the teachers waved at them to go inside, but the ladies just jeered at her. My teacher finally walked over to talk to them on the porch. She came back red-faced and flustered.

The ladies caught on that we were watching, and apparently didn't like the extra attention we caused. They began wearing witch costumes to scare us—pointy hats and all. If we ventured too close or lingered at the low chain-link fence separating the playground from their house, they cackled at us until we ran away. They chased a classmate with a broom when he was brave enough to step over the fence and approach the house. We sure kept our distance after that, but we still watched. The teachers steered us further down the playground to play.

Uncle Bert, who was a few years older, heard us talking about the witches living next to the school. "It's a cat-house," he said with authority, and explained what it meant. We stared in stunned disbelief.

Hussies, next to our school? Right next to where we went to church? Impossible!

Bert said he would prove it. We collected bottles and pooled our deposit money with his allowance money. After about a month we had five dollars. We stood on the shoulder of the road across from the house to see if he would really do it. We wagered our future allowances on it while we watched. The place was already having a detrimental affect on us.

Bert knocked on the door and talked to the lady. He never would reveal what she said, but he returned with a beet-red face and all his money.

Not long afterward, we watched from the playground as the ladies were loaded into patrol cars. They didn't look happy, but my teacher smirked and snickered. She was the last one to get any satisfaction out of the situation.

33

PENANCE

Pawpaw let my Dad use his 1951 Studebaker Commander Starlight V8 Coupe for about a year when I was very young. I remember the curious lap blanket cord that stretched across the back of the front seat, and the special Venetian blinds that kept the blinding sun out of the glass that wrapped completely around the car. It was quiet and smooth, and it provided trouble-free transportation for many years. That is, until Jake and I did an experiment.

The car was just 16 years old when Pawpaw parked it on the oval dirt track that doubled as our softball field. Pawpaw had scraped us a nice go-kart track using his ancient Gibson tractor, and the bullet-nosed Studebaker sat there for a few months with some kind of mechanical problem.

Jake and I admired that car. It had long, pointy fenders, and the front came to a point that held a silver bullet between the headlights. It looked like a fighter plane. It even had a propeller than spun on the center of the bullet, and the two-piece grille made the corners of a smile. For those too young to remember seeing one on the road, it was just like the Little Blue Car from the cartoon; the kind of car Fozzie Bear drove in the Muppet Movie.

We had gotten in trouble for a few accidental BB chips in the glass of some of the cars parked around the farm, the results of ricochets. Our Daisy rifles had been locked away, and we were bored. We practiced throwing rocks for a while, then located some old inner tubes and cut strips. We cut off two Y-shaped branches and made powerful slingshots.

We were unsuccessful at hitting any birds, but we could hit stationary targets such as tin cans with ease. As we wandered the yard seeking new targets, we paused next to the stalwart coupe. "Safety glass," Jake read off the windshield. "I wonder if it really is unbreakable?" We bantered back and forth for quite some time. We noticed an earlier BB chip in the windshield that had not penetrated. "Let's see," said Jake, and he tossed a medium-sized rock at the windshield. It just bounced off, not even leaving a mark.

"See, told you it was." Growing bolder, he launched a rock with his slingshot that deflected at a low angle, scratching the glass but leaving no crack.

"I guess it really is unbreakable," I opined, and drew back my slingshot to its full extent. When I loosed my missile, the rock left a spider-web crack as big as a silver dollar. We were both shocked, and didn't know what to do. Since the damage was done, we decided to see just how tough the glass was. By the time we were done, the entire windshield had fractured into quarter-inch squares but layers of tinted film inside still held it together. We panicked and ran home.

Pawpaw came to our place, mad as a hornet. He dragged our Dad and the two of us to the scene of the crime. We cried as we explained what had happened. "Get me a switch," Granny demanded. I walked slowly to the hedgerow, and broke off a long but skinny branch. Granny gave each of us a dozen whacks across the butt and legs. It stung—a lot. We would eventually learn that the skinny branches cut a lot more, and to choose a bigger branch, since its blunt whacks were hardly felt at all. Such discipline was reserved for the most destructive acts, or doing something lethally stupid.

I am now in my third year of penance for this decades-old crime. My partner PJ bought me a 1951 Studebaker 4-door three years ago as a retirement present. I chose the car because of its unusual looks, its very advanced engineering features, and to make up for a stupid act I had regretted for four decades. I told Pawpaw before he passed away how sorry I was, and that I wanted to get my own Bullet-Nose one day.

I've done all the work myself except having the transmission rebuilt. It has an automatic transmission with a lock-up torque converter, a feature the Big Three would not introduce for another three decades. Three summers and two winters spent carefully going through the car's mechanics and electrical system, working on a concrete patio next to the house. Blistering in the summer and working until my fingers were too cold to hold the tools in the winter.

The car runs like a watch when I pull out the starter handle, and I marvel at how smooth and durable a sixty-year-old car can be. Bringing it back to its full 1951 potential brings me satisfaction. I love bringing low-tech things like tube radios back to life, and they will work as well as they did new with a bit of effort. In many cases, that level of performance is quite high.

There are some transgressions that just can't be fixed, some words too hurtful for any apology, but I can do my best to correct one blunder. I have said a few things that couldn't be taken back, and caused damage that can't be undone. The best I can do is to avoid such actions in the future, and finish making one Studebaker whole again.

34

EARLY MORNING PICK-ME-UP

Uncle Bert was a newly licensed driver when he came visiting our place in Walnut Grove. When we'd left the Jackson place in Riverdale, Dad had bought a large mobile home, and it was certainly mobile.

First we moved it to a lovely grassy field on the outskirts of Monroe. He dragged it all the way back to Riverdale after just a few weeks when racial unrest in Walton County erupted that was worse than the Atlanta drug problem we'd escaped. He got permission to keep it on the back of Pawpaw's farm for the summer of '68. Next, he bought an eight-acre patch of farmland alongside a creek in Walnut Grove next to the old Canon farmhouse. We bought the first parcel of the old Canon Farm, in a district that came to be known as The Baby Farms because of the original advertisement extolling the large parcels as "Baby Farms." I didn't notice an unusual birth rate, but a few residents tried to squelch the use of the name after fifteen years or so.

Dad parked it beneath a twisted old pine, near the dirt road and close to the creek. This proved untenable. The septic tank crew hit water just three feet down, and the septic system was useless.

He had the trailer moved to the highest ground on the eight acres, next to a young sweetgum tree. It had a nice view overlooking the creek. It was good that he moved it anyway, since the creek that normally ran two or three inches deep and maybe four feet wide turned into a torrent eight feet deep and fifty yards wide when Hurricane Camille visited the following year.

We had survived racial unrest, a hurricane, and being uprooted several times. But we were still struggling for financial survival. I had cost just forty-nine dollars for when I was born. When my little sister Rachael was born just four years later, the two weeks of labor Mother endured had cost them over two thousand. Dad was on the hook with a finance company. It was a struggle to make the land and trailer payments and still keep up with the loan.

Things were a bit on edge the day that Bert drove up the gravel driveway into the field that was our front yard. He grinned when he got out, "Now I'm legal!" He'd driven around on some of the country roads before. Actually, he'd begun learning to drive at twelve, driving us around the go-kart track in an old Chevrolet that Pawpaw let him practice with. But now he could go as far as his gas money would allow him.

In his excitement, Bert forgot that the hand brake didn't work on the '49 Ford pickup he left in Neutral. There was a loud "bang" that shook the trailer to its foundation, and the lights flickered. I had been reading in my top bunk. I ran outside to see what had happened. I thought a power transformer had exploded or something the way the lights had dimmed. I saw the pickup nosed into the house and examined the crease he'd left along the bottom of the trailer. I was poking my head carefully underneath to see if Bert had pushed it off the foundation blocks when I heard a bellow above my head, "Don't let 'em pull it!"

Dad had been asleep in the room at the far end of the trailer. We looked up, and the bedroom window was billowing white. At first I thought it was curtains moving, but then we got a better look. The small aluminum window frame was filled with derriere. Lots of it. Dad was trying to stuff himself out the window, butt-first, all the while hollering, "Don't let them pull it!"

Dad tried three or four times, but never managed to exit that window. We laughed until we cried watching him. The truck and trailer were fine, and the finance company wouldn't get the trailer until several months later.

35

COLD AS A WELL DIGGER

It's surprisingly warm outside for Groundhog Day—shirtsleeve weather. A senior politician's invention of the Internet caused huge demands on electricity to power all the computers that would never have been built without the 'Net. Not to mention all the carbon from the actual production of all those toys. But there have been times when I was cold. One of the coldest was in the middle of June, when we hand-dug our well.

We'd moved the trailer to the outskirts of Monroe. We placed it on higher ground in a field where chest-high grass waved at passers-by. We didn't have our own creek, but the neighbors across the road had a creek to play in. We got the power hooked up, and we set about looking for water.

We could have called in a well-drilling company, but it was too expensive. My Dad called in family to help, and people arrived with shovels. Pawpaw used two bent metal rods to dowse for water and got a good indication not far from the trailer. Dad and Bert took turns with the shovel, making a hole four feet square. We always dug square wells. Round ones got oblong and it was hard to keep the hole straight. Four feet was just big enough for a small man to dig down as far as necessary. Often small boys would be sent down the hole once it became too uncomfortable for the adults.

They dug for two days. Dad did a lot of the early work, but he was too large to fit into the hole as it sank farther into the ground. Bert took over. Once it was head-deep, we rigged a windlass above the hole to lift the buckets of dirt, cranking a handle driven into a log to wind up the rope. The bucket carried the dirt to the surface and transported the digger up and down the hole. It was an uneasy ride with one foot inside the bucket, trying to hold a shovel while you tried to maintain your balance by holding onto the rope.

At about eighteen feet, Bert came up from the depths with a big grin and a large quartz rock. He was excited. He pointed to the streaks in the rock, asking Pawpaw if it could be gold. Pawpaw studied it intently, and said maybe—gold had been mined in large quantities just fifty miles north in Dahlonega and at many other Georgia locations. Pawpaw knew his gold. He and his father had worked in the Hog Mountain mine in Alabama. It was a quarter-mile down and two miles back just to get to work. A fellow miner once kicked up a two-ounce nugget when they were having lunch on the surface.

Eventually, even teenaged Bert tired. Jake took over for a while. He reached a trickle of water, but it wasn't gushing in. He had done enough, and it was my turn. I stepped into the bucket with a long-handled spade and steadied myself on the rope. You used a long handled shovel down there: there was no room to stoop over with a short shovel. I still wobbled back and forth unsteadily in the bucket. Worms and tree roots passed my eye level as I descended, then rocky soil; then it was all red clay. The clay was damp, and I wanted to finish my work and get back up. Clay holes and ditches are prone to caving in on you.

The light was dim at the bottom, but I could see just well enough to work. I stood upright and took small bites off the floor by my feet; sending up bucket after bucket of damp, then wet clay. The work wasn't that hard but it was uncomfortable. The shovel could only take bites of about half a shovelful at that angle. I had to lean back against the cold, damp wall, moving from one side of the hole to the other to dig on the side where I had been standing. I penetrated another three feet beyond Jake's stopping place. There was a steady stream coming in now, from two directions. It was late in the afternoon. I could barely see any more at the bottom, and the tiny spot of light at the top of the hole was not as bright as before. They hauled me back up.

I asked them how deep we'd dug. Twenty-five feet, about six times my own height. I was stuck at four feet tall for three years, with a raspy voice like Froggy on the Little Rascals. At that point, I thought my height and voice were permanent.

I learned an appreciation for the meaning of, "Cold as a well digger's butt." In a hole that size, you have no choice but to lean against one side of the hole and work the shovel across from your feet. I had a greater respect for well diggers, and for the gold miners of

Georgia and Alabama who drove such holes to the water table, sometimes eighty feet or more through the clay.

"Cold as a well digger's butt." It really does get cold, trust me. I don't recall a TV weatherman actually using the phrase, though I once heard an Atlanta radio announcer proclaim that it was so cold that there wasn't a pawnshop sign left intact on Moreland Avenue. As descriptive as those phrases are, I'm looking forward to the day when TV weathermen forecast the winter weather with the assistance of an on-camera witch.

36

WE ARE INVADED

For a long time, there were only four or five homes on the three-mile stretch of Old Georgia 138 that meandered past the old Canon farm. We had the run of the place, along with the deer, foxes and snakes.

Our first neighbor took the parcel across the road on a picturesque spot overlooking the creek. He struggled for days to get his mobile home situated, but the trees and the lay of the land worked against him. He finally ended up with the view he wanted from his window, even if it did mean that the uphill end of the trailer rested on the dirt and the end with the front door hovered nine feet off the ground. Our second neighbor took the parcel behind us, sandwiched between our eight acres that faced the dirt road and the paved state highway behind us. They were from New York, and we were fascinated with them.

There were Yankees encamped in our back yard, with only three strands of barbed wire protecting us. Granny reacted to the news with consternation, and having no cavalry at her disposal, she sent out spies. We introduced ourselves and watched as Tracy laid concrete blocks. He built a sturdy house for his wife and their children Bruce, Bryan, Lynne, and Becky. It was a no-frills affair: even the interior walls were bare concrete block.

They talked funny but seemed friendly enough. They'd not yet stolen any horses or burned any crops, and we reported such to Granny. Tracy planted a big garden and brought in a steer the kids called Gulliver. We reported that they were hard-working folk, and had never once uttered, "That's not how we used to do it up North." We decided they were all right and took them under our wing. They'd be susceptible to the hazards of living in the country. We helped them lay the last concrete blocks and get the roof on before cold weather set in.

They had a good-sized garden and it produced well. I watched in horror as their daughter Lynne plucked the squash blossoms and deposited them into her bucket. "What are you *doing*?" I asked, "Now you won't get any squash!" She smiled and said they were going to eat the blossoms. "But you'll get way more squash if you leave the blossoms alone!" When we laughed about this at home over dinner, we concluded that these misguided Northerners were going to need a lot of help. They certainly talked faster than they could possibly be thinking.

We rode the same school bus and attended many of the same classes. Lynne and I even shared a few kisses once. There was still a lot of tsk-tsk in our discussions about them. Much to our amusement, Bruce and Bryan would saddle Gulliver and ride him around their six acres. We had fun exploring the creek and woods together. Bruce had a bullwhip, and was so skilled he could smack a spider with it at ten feet or more. We showed them dangers they were unfamiliar with. What copperheads and moccasins looked like and where they were likely to live; how to avoid ticks and black scorpions. Things you could eat in the woods and things that would kill you.

I was stunned the first time I saw Mrs. D. with Becky on a leash. I thought it was cruel to treat a four-year-old like that. She'd tether Becky's chest harness to the bedpost while she did housework or to a post outside when she was gardening. We were actually a bit angry about it. We were, until the day Becky arrived unannounced at the spring Dad had dug out of the creek bank for our drinking water. The hole was four feet across and five or six feet deep. Doris, Jake and I were using Granny's tea strainer to dip tadpoles from it to examine.

We never heard her coming. Becky walked right over the edge of it, dropping feet-first into the water. After a one-second hesitation Doris grabbed Becky's hair floating at the surface, and together we lifted her straight up. She was heavy. She coughed a little. We turned her upside down and bounced her up and down a few times, and she expelled the rest of the water. We were in shock as we marched her home. We agreed that Mrs. D. hadn't been mean in putting her on a tether. There were things in the country that could kill a four-year-old if they weren't savvy.

Bryan was the one fondest of Gulliver. He kept the steer groomed and fed, and did manage to keep the saddle on him for short rides before it would loosen and slide off. Gulliver didn't seem to mind.

They were largely vegetarian, so when Bryan came home one day to the smell of steaks cooking it was an unusual treat. The all ate heartily. I still don't understand why Bryan's father waited until they had finished before telling the kids that that Gulliver had joined them for dinner. Bryan took it really hard.

We got to be pretty good friends. Uncle Dave even worked for Tracy in the construction business for a while. We moved, and they moved, but we visited them at their new place a few times. To my surprise, I literally bumped into Bryan some years later when we both attended Mercer University in Macon. We reconnected for a while but lost touch again.

In spite of our differences, we learned from each other and we broke down some misconceptions. But I still prefer squash to squash blossoms.

37

ANKLE DEEP MONEY

Pawpaw bought the old Canon farmhouse next door to us and moved in soon after we settled on the creek. It was a beautiful two-story frame house built in 1848. It was easy to step out the upstairs bedroom windows onto the front porch roof. Jake and I liked to sit out there and watch the world go by on the dirt road that still bore State Highway 138 signs. The interior walls were wide pine planks, most of them unpainted. Many of those boards were over two feet wide. We played in a sort of secret passage between an upstairs bedroom wall and the eaves where the builders had put shelves and pegs for storage. The two big chimneys were made of rough-cut granite from the nearby outcroppings, and the well was lined with granite blocks with steps cut into them.

If you walked the dirt road past our trailer and crossed the plank bridge spanning the creek, the first house on the right was the old Canon Farm supervisor's home. It sat down in a narrow flat between the road edge and a branch behind it, its eaves roughly even with the road's edge. It was an attractive house even though it had never been painted in its lifetime. It was empty when we first arrived, but we visited the kids who moved in later.

We were exploring with them not long after they moved in. We peeked into an old tack shed across the road. The shed sat alongside a driveway that ran from the dirt road back through the woods to the Canon family cemetery on the hillside. The shed was unpainted pine, not very large but tall. We saw only some hay and some old leather straps downstairs. There wasn't a true upstairs; it was more like a shelf you could walk on. There weren't stairs, but there were rungs nailed to the wall you could climb up.

We hauled ourselves up there and looked around. There were a couple of harness parts still hanging on pegs in the wall, but we got excited about what lay scattered on the floor. It was ankle deep in old newspapers and old money. Confederate money. Ones, fives, hundreds. There were enough bills to fill a large steamer trunk. Someone's lost fortune had lain there undisturbed for a hundred and five years.

The bills were odd shades of pink, and big—half again as big as bills are today. The designs on them were quite ornate, attractive in a way. Most were whole but mice had chewed the corners off a few of them. The newspapers were in rougher condition, but you could easily read the news of both Northern and Southern victories.

Kids growing up in Georgia in the Sixties and Seventies were fascinated by old things; the relics and scars of war at our feet; the rumors of lost treasure. You could still see a few of the rails that Sherman's troops twisted around trees even when I was in college. MARTA subway workers digging in the edge of Underground Atlanta near the Capitol found eight million dollars (face value) in Civil War era gold coins in 1979—four pickup loads. Radio news reports said the workers got to keep a few coins, but the fate of the rest was never revealed. Kids in Jonesboro still kick up Minnie balls from the trenches that cut across their back yards. The last Union and Confederate widows died in 2003 and 2004, respectively—our history is not all that far removed from us even now.

I looked over the bills. We scooped them up and tossed some around. But no one took any. They weren't ours to keep.

I had a fight with one of the kids. He was mean, and he had deliberately run his bike right into me at full speed. It was a long time before I visited again: about two years. Our group watched cartoons at their place for a couple of hours, then went out to explore. We checked on the tack shed we'd examined two years earlier. I had started collecting inexpensive Wheat pennies as a hobby. I was curious about the Confederate money we'd seen. If it was still there, I planned to ask around about who owned the shed.

I wish there had been someone to talk to sooner. The mice had taken a toll in the months since we'd visited. The biggest scraps left were the corners of banknotes. The mice had nested and chewed them to pieces.

Today, I wish I'd had the chance to ask about the ownership of the old newspapers and money before the mice destroyed them, but I wouldn't change my actions. I'm sure a lot of people had stumbled upon the money in the hundred years it laid there. Some left it because Confederate money was of minimal value; others left it because it belonged to someone. For us kids, it was respect for what belonged to other people.

38

THE FALL OF '69

I was eight the year I broke my arm. The creek had just returned to its banks from the Hurricane Camille flooding. We were enjoying a warm August day during what had been a chilly summer. The summer of '69 had bordered on jacket weather, with dire predictions of a coming Ice Age brought on by the Greenhouse Effect.

I climbed the rungs square-nailed to the barn stall. The barn was large, befitting the size of the old Canon farm. I thought I'd find my siblings playing in the stacks of hay bales, but they were nowhere to be found. Before I could ease back down the ladder, I was startled. I thought it was a hornet, an ill-tempered creature capable of knocking you to the ground if it hit you. Without thinking, I ran.

The square bales were stacked high, with a walkway down the center. There were two holes in the floor that permitted dropping hay directly to the stalls below. I found one of those holes.

I remember being eye level with the floor and headed downward. I wasn't scared exactly—we sometimes jumped from the upstairs loading door at the end of the barn onto stacks of hay. But there were no haystacks in the stall below. This was going to hurt, and I expected to have the wind knocked out of me. I was not prepared for what actually happened. I saw the floor beam rising up to meet me. The floor was long gone, but one beam remained. I couldn't change my flight path. I landed on it, my right arm pinned between my body and the wooden beam. At least I'd missed the nails.

I regained my wind. My arm stung but it didn't hurt all that bad. But it looked funny. I sought out my Uncle Bert's opinion. He said with conviction, "Yep, you broke it. See how it hangs down at an angle behind the wrist?" I nodded. "Let's go see Maw."

I was calm up to this point. I'd shed maybe three tears because the arm smarted a bit. Granny went into a full meltdown when she saw the arm. She stamped her feet and wailed, "Get him to the Vet! He's broke his arm!"

Bert and I laughed. The *Vet?* Granny spun in circles, then she sent a runner next door. Mother pulled the Falcon wagon between the big poles on either side of the driveway that still held up the "Canon Farm" sign. She left the car running. Granny claimed shotgun, and I was given the back seat, with a pillow to rest my arm. We sped off toward the hospital in Monroe, ten miles distant, with Granny still squealing, "Get him to the Vet!"

The doctor looked at the arm and said it was certainly broken. He didn't immediately try to set it. The X-rays showed that my weight had split both bones lengthwise, and snapped both of them across the wrist. He said it would be tricky, but he could set it.

I watched the screen as he moved bones back into position with a big needle. He worked as gingerly as he could.

"Those should stay, but you'll have to take it easy for a while. Let's put a cast on it." He grabbed a bucket, rolls of gauze, and bags of Plaster of Paris. He could have had a fine career in drywall if he'd wanted. He dipped the strips of gauze into the bucket. They were warm. As he laid each one in place, he smeared a thin layer of plaster on it. It was very low-tech. He gave me a bandage roll to hold to keep my hand in a natural position. By the time he finished, I had a heavy chunk of damp plaster from the middle of my fingers to well above my elbow. I'd have to use a sling to hold the weight of it.

"How long does it have to stay on?" I asked. He explained that it would be six or eight weeks. I'd have to keep it dry, meaning sponge baths instead of showers. He set an appointment for a follow-up in two weeks.

The break hadn't hurt much at all; maybe I was in shock. But it ached as it healed, especially at night. And itched, especially after my big sister caught me unawares and poured breadcrumbs into the cast. The biggest challenge was learning to write left-handed when I started school two weeks later, which I managed.

The Doc was satisfied with his work and my progress two weeks later. I'm glad he discussed the injury with me directly, which made me feel grown up. He corrected the only problem I mentioned—that the cast was a bit tight at the fingers. He pulled a quarter from his pocket and pried against the plaster until the edges cracked enough to suit him. The tools of the medical trade aren't always complicated.

He did good work. I regained full use of the arm, and the only ill effect was that when the foul-smelling dead skin peeled after he removed the cast, I dug at it until I left some scars. I could finally scratch that itch.

It's amazing how much damage you can do when you only <u>think</u> you know what's going on. Halfway down to the ground, I had realized the "hornet" was only a dragonfly that had flown past my ear, but its approach from behind had spooked me.

39

A NEW COUSIN ARRIVES

Granny was an excitable woman. Fern was great with child, her second. She was miserable and eager to get it over with. She had followed Granny to the Canon Farm place, and Pawpaw renovated the small barn behind the main house for her family to live in. Near lunchtime one Thursday, the time arrived. She told Granny that her water had broken and went to the porch to await transportation. This was her second child and Fern was quite calm and confident in her weeks of advance preparation. Granny, on the other hand, reacted as if the sky was falling.

She tried to follow the well-prepared checklist Fern had reviewed with her several days earlier. She gathered Fern's clothes. She found the diaper bag in its pre-staged spot in the living room. She picked up Fern's young son Larry and readied him for the trip. She awoke Bert upstairs to drive, and he warmed the up the car while she gathered Larry's playthings for the trip. The car's choke didn't work right, and it always took five minutes to warm up enough to move. Bert was compliant, but not entirely awake. He had been working night shift at the cotton mill since he'd left high school.

The wooden screen door made a loud smack as its spring pulled it back. Granny loaded Larry into the car and filled the back seat with enough materiel for a long military campaign. She barked a constant stream of orders to Bert, mostly to hurry up. He dropped the car into First gear and slung gravel as they headed for the hospital in Monroe. Their dust settled on the expectant mother still sitting on the porch.

Fern was somewhat deflated sitting on the porch. She was bemused, but it still hurt. Everyone else was at work. It was unusually quiet. One of the best things about living there was the quiet. The most noticeable noise was the wind through the leaves. Often it was so quiet you could hear the feet of a rabbit when it hopped across the grass. It was interrupted maybe seven or eight times a day by a car moving slowly down the gravel road. The mail plane left at dawn, buzzing slowly overhead and it made its return trip about three in the afternoon. You could hear the tire and engine noise of a single car out on the main highway several miles prior to its arrival and for a good three miles after its departure. There wasn't even a mail truck—we were so remote we had to drive to the county seat once a week to pick up the mail; there weren't enough people to make a rural route. She felt very alone.

She'd sat there in labor for about twenty minutes when my mother pulled the Falcon station wagon in to drop off some butter. Mother was returning from town with a load of water and a few groceries. The Canon farm well had proved insufficient for three families, and we hauled in water in gallon jugs while we saved up to get our own well drilled.

Fern smiled and explained the problem. Mother helped Fern into the car and they made a leisurely ten-mile drive, arriving at the hospital about half an hour after Granny's advance force. The delivery went fine, and she returned home in two or three days with a fine baby girl.

40

YOSEMITE DAVE

Uncle Dave bought a purple Triumph Bonneville 650 motorcycle in 1970, one of the fastest production bikes on the road at the time. Although he drove it way too fast, he never had an accident. He'd had the bike about two years when he gathered a group of friends for the great road trip they said they'd take one day.

There was little planning or preparation involved. Dave packed a sleeping bag and a road atlas, and a metal box to contain matches for a campfire. I think they decided on a Wednesday to depart that same weekend for the trip out West. There were six bikes and one pickup truck in case a bike broke down.

They rode hard, arriving in Yellowstone after just three days. They rode around the park admiring the sights and settled down with sandwiches near the Old Faithful geyser. It quickly got boring. His friend Mike timed the eruptions with his wristwatch. "I'll be back," was all he said.

Mike returned in the pickup with an old steering wheel he'd plucked off an abandoned tractor he'd seen a mile or so outside the park. He picked a spot just off the sight line of the tourists and pushed the shaft of the steering wheel into the soft ground.

His accomplice Dave stood beside him in coveralls and a railroad hat, officiously studying his pocket watch. When it was time for Old Faithful to spew forth, Mike cranked the steering wheel furiously counter-clockwise after Dave hollered, "Up!" When it approached time for the water to fall, Dave shouted, "Down!" and Mike cranked it as fast as he could clockwise, grunting and making a big production of it.

Tourists began to notice. They were close enough to hear, "I knew it was fake!" a few times. Tourists stared over in their direction before stomping off to their cars. They'd been at their task for about half an hour before a couple of German tourists wandered over for a closer look. Mike and Dave didn't say anything to them as they diligently assisted Old Faithful. The tourists scowled and went over to talk to a park ranger.

Mike and Dave were invited to leave by a park ranger who was even more steamed than the nearby geyser. He saw no humor in their charade. They made a hasty retreat, never to return.

41

MEET THE GALLWAYS

Uncle Dave sometimes hung out with a family of moonshiners for the entertainment value. There were only three broadcast TV stations back then, plus the two snowy ones on the UHF dial. One fall afternoon he drove the five miles to see what they were up to. The last time he had visited, they had discussed killing some hogs. When the conversation turned to making Brunswick Stew the old-timey way, Dave had asked them to call him the next time they cooked it up. It was one thing to read about mountain skills in *The Foxfire Book*, but seeing those skills put to use was a rare treat. Many of those old ways had been set aside when Pawpaw moved out of Alabama's back hills.

For the uninitiated, Brunswick stew is a semi-sweet delight served at better Southern bar-b-que joints. The meat is slow-cooked, shredded really fine and mixed with corn. It's not a meal in itself, but it makes a perfect side dish for bar-b-que.

Dave followed the scent when he stepped out of his car, finding Candler Gallway and the others gathered around two iron cauldrons just inside the pinewoods below Candler's old frame house. Hog-killing time was a happy time, and the contents of the Mason jars had made them even more jovial. "Dave, let me show you how it's *really* done," beamed Candler as he handed Dave his own jar. His brother Aaron was dumping a large pot of freshly shelled corn on top of the stew. "Been slow cookin' since this mornin'". He stirred it into the stew with a boat paddle. "'Bout another hour," he announced.

Several scraggly dogs darted in and out of their feet. Talk was drowned out by the squeal of dogs yelping as they fought over hog entrails. Dogs too timid to win hog scraps lapped up the stew right out of the pot. When Dave shooed the dogs from the pot, Candler just laughed and told him that, "The fire will kill any germs."

The sensory overload overwhelmed Dave. He told them he was headed up to the house to the bathroom. What he really wanted now was a sandwich. He hadn't eaten all day in anticipation of home-cooked stew. He exited the bathroom and headed for the kitchen, hungry for something with a little less dog spit in it.

He stopped dead at the kitchen door, staring at the monkey sitting amongst the dishes on the table. It grinned at him and continued doing what it was doing...and Dave's mother wasn't there to cover his eyes or divert his attention. Dave blinked several times and lost his appetite entirely.

Dave sat drinking quietly with Candler and his brother Aaron as they told stories and stirred the cauldrons. Fall hog killing was a kind of harvest celebration. The Gallways were so caught up in it that they didn't notice Dave's long silence.

Finally, a nephew slid down the steep back yard trail into the edge of the woods carrying a baloney sandwich and an RC Cola. With a sloppy grin, he asked Aaron, "How long you had that monkey?"

Dave had never been so relieved. He'd been scared to move, uncertain whether to go to the emergency room. Maybe the liquor *wasn't* contaminated. Maybe his mind was still intact. Someone *else* had seen the monkey, too!

Dave thanked his hosts for showing off their old-time skills, and for the company. He eased his Austin-Healy toward home. He didn't even tell us that story for another couple of months...after he quit drinking for good.

42

OATMEAL DOES A BODY GOOD

Dave stopped in to check on Coosa one afternoon. He finally found him at the home of Coosa's brother Arthur. The place reeked of a two-week drunk. They had a set of bunk beds and a big couch on the perimeter of the front room. The kitchen lay just beyond.

Dave didn't even get his coat off before Arthur raised up enough to rasp, "Dave, check on Torey. He said he wasn't feeling good." Neither of the moonshiners was in any condition to get up.

The table hadn't been cleared in a long time. Dirty dishes occupied every seat. There was a large plate of oatmeal on one side of the table that had flies hovering around it. They hovered, because Torey had already landed in it. Several days ago. And he smelled a bit ripe.

Dave held back a bit and asked them, "How long since you talked to him?" "Oh, he hasn't moved in a couple of days." "He don't talk much anyways."

Coosa got one eye open and slurred, "We tried feeding him some oatmeal on Thursday, but he don't want to eat anything." It was now Saturday afternoon.

Dave laid the back of his hand on Torey's neck. Cold. He slid up Torey's sleeve. No pulse. "Arthur, he's dead--been dead a while."

"Oh, my word. He was such a good man, a good friend." No one had yet risen, least of all Torey.

"Should we call the doctor?" Coosa inquired, finally raising upright. "No," Dave advised, "We have to call the law. You have to when there's a death. No doctor's gonna help him now."

Coosa and Arthur were alert now. "No, no, don't call the law. We'll take care of him. We got a family cemetery just up the road."

Dave's eyes widened, and he told the older men in his most confident tone, "Hey, I ain't goin' to jail for not reporting it. We have to call the sheriff." Despite their pleas, Dave dialed the sheriff's office.

While Dave spoke to the sheriff's office Arthur went through the pockets of Torey's overalls. He pocketed the wad of bills from his billfold and the singles from his shirt pocket before he returned his wallet.

"Law's on the way. They said it's not a big deal but they still have to come out so he can get a death certificate," Dave told them. Coosa straightened up the house, putting away the mason jars of liquor. No need for additional excitement today.

A half-hour later, the coroner's wagon rolled quietly up the dirt driveway. Before they could reach the door, an agitated Arthur slid a ten-dollar bill into Torey's shirt pocket then retreated to the far side of the living room.

Dave explained the situation as he knew it. The coroner asked Coosa and Arthur the same questions, trying to pin down the time of death. While they were interviewing Coosa, an anxious Arthur blurted out, "He was stone-cold dead when I checked him…and he only had ten dollars in his pocket."

They told them the death seemed to be from natural causes, but that they would have to give them an official cause of death in a couple of days. They wheeled Torey away on a gurney. As Torey crossed the threshold for the last time, Arthur shifted from foot to foot, lamenting, "Sure is awful he died like that. At least he died with friends. He only had <u>ten dollars</u>."

The drunks had sobered up. Dave reassured them that the law had no other interest in them, which calmed them down. Still, they were shaken up and chattered about how good a man Torey had been. As they got dressed to go visit Torey's family, Dave seized the opportunity to extract himself.

A few weeks later a policeman stopped by Coosa's place with news from the coroner. Torey had died quietly of a heart attack and had not suffered. The oatmeal had been too little, too late.

43

ICE CREAM

I was nine when we moved again, to a tarpaper shack at the end of a dirt street in Monroe, next to the airport. Money was still tight in 1970. My mother got a sales job selling fire equipment. She sold a couple of fire trucks but the commissions never materialized. Jake and I strapped fire extinguishers on our bikes, trying to sell them door-to-door, but we got no sales. My Dad got a welding supply route, driving a large flat bed truck filled with tanks of oxygen, acetylene, nitrogen and argon. His commissions were spotty, and a lot of customers just kept the tanks until they were empty and stiffed him.

His parent company finally intervened in June. He got paid for many of the delinquent accounts and his commissions were brought up to date. It was time for a summer celebration. He drove us the ten miles north to Winder. We swam at Fort Yargo state park and marveled at the bullet holes in the 1792 fort. Before we headed home, he stopped at the Pet ice cream company. "Pick out any two flavors you want," he told us.

We were excited. Before specialty ice cream was available in stores, fresh ice cream from the creamery was the best you could get. We discussed the choices earnestly, settling on butter pecan and vanilla. Dad and Mother loaded four kids and both two-gallon commercial drums of ice cream into our Falcon station wagon.

We cooked out that afternoon: hot dogs and marshmallows. We knocked a softball around. We had ice cream, but not a lot—we planned to make it last.

Around two in the morning, thunder shook the house. Lightning struck the trees nearby in rapid succession. The bright light and noise made it impossible to sleep. We were already awake when Dad gathered us all into the kitchen around three o'clock.

"Here, there's no sense in wasting it. Eat all you want--as much as you can." He gave each child a big spoon. The storm had knocked out the power, and the ice cream was beginning to thaw inside the 1950s vintage freezer. We rubbed our eyes and dug in.

I suppose I ate three-fourths of a gallon before hitting the "full" mark. I rested, but there would be no second round for me. I got a little queasy and knew I'd get sick if I continued. When the last child complained that they could eat no more, we were sent back to bed.

The next morning, the remaining ice cream had melted into soup. The freezer didn't begin humming again until eight o'clock. I skipped breakfast.

It was one of the nicest things our parents ever did for us. Surprisingly, my favorite ice cream is still butter pecan.

44

THE GREAT LAUNCH

My Dad's welding supply truck was a tall flatbed with stake sides for cinching down the high-pressure gas cylinders. We were a little afraid of it. He explained how much pressure the tanks held and took out an old car key to show us what compressed nitrogen could do. The key frosted, and when he thumped it, the key shattered into dozens of pieces.

After he brought home a company newsletter describing a recent industrial accident at the plant where he picked up his tanks, we were even more afraid of it. Someone had painted over a cracked oxygen tank, and it split open when they filled it. The worker next to the tank was killed instantly when it let loose. Another worker on the far end of the warehouse was knocked through a concrete block wall, knocking off his arms and legs. A third was decapitated. The safety bulletin even had pictures of the damaged wall. The company took safety seriously, and put the brutal details out to employees for good reason.

I used to worry about those tanks. Dad said that they needed to stay cool, and he tried to park in the shade when he could. When he couldn't, he parked the truck a good distance from the house.

I was playing with my little sister alongside the house one Sunday. It was really hot that August, for days on end. We were lethargic. I sat my sister up onto the propane tank next to the house just as a loud boom echoed across the yard, followed by a deafening 'whoosh.' I froze for a second, but once I realized we had not exploded the propane tank, I yanked her to the ground. I dragged her behind me by the hand. We peeked around the corner of the house and saw a white vapor jet shooting twenty feet into the air from an oxygen tank strapped in the middle of the full load.

"Run!" I yelled but lost my grip on her hand. I figured the safest place was in the woods, and I ran so fast my heels smacked into my butt. I dove headfirst over the low barbed wire fence and rolled a couple of times. I lay flat for a time listening to the 'whoosh.' The burst tank had not set off any others, but I was taking no chances. I moved quickly down the trails and out to the main road a quarter-mile away.

I sat at the main road for a good fifteen or twenty minutes after the whooshing stopped. I picked my way back through the privet forest and climbed over the fence. My Dad and brother were looking around the yard. Finally, Jake came up with the cap. The long threaded cap was about eight inches tall, and most of it was buried in the soft garden soil. I'd heard a loud whistle when the tank's valve let go, but hadn't known it was the cap streaking toward the sky. I don't know how far up it flew, but it landed with a lot of force.

Even though I rode along with Dad to help with deliveries the following summer, I never got comfortable in that truck. I guess that useful discomfort is why they give ammunition ships names like "USS Nitro."

45

THE PIGLETS

Mother had a soft spot for animals. She was helping Dad with welding supply deliveries, hauling some of the smaller items in our car. A farmer discussed his pigs with her and lamented that he'd have to cull some runts. She returned home with four pink piglets.

They were small and weak, and two of them died within a week despite us bottle- feeding them around the clock. The other two grew to a good size on a diet of table scraps and "wheat shorts," which was some kind of bran product.

Of course they would get out of their pen. In the beginning, it was great fun catching them. They were surprisingly fast. It broke up the monotony.

John Robinson ran a store out on Snow's Mill Road, the old route from Monroe to Athens. It sat in the fork of the road, with his well-drilling business behind. Mr. Robinson was a pleasant man who enjoyed the people who stopped by, even the ones who just sat on the porch to tell stories and sip RC Cola. Not much had changed since his grandfather first opened the place; his faded photo had a place of honor above the door. Robinson sold a lot of baloney, thick or thin-cut as you chose. There were always two hoops of cheddar on the counter, the best-tasting cheese anywhere. He had locally grown vegetables and meats. There were two long, deep freezers for the ice cream. You slid the covers back and leaned way in for a treat. They were old but they worked fine.

We were living about a half-mile down the road, an easy bike ride. We were used to hard living: when we played rock, paper, scissors, we used real rocks, real paper, and real scissors. But when we tried to garden, the hard clay was too much for us kids to hoe. The hogs grew large, but not fat. Catching an escaped hog had already been a two-person job: one to distract and another to catch the back legs. The hogs had grown to over a hundred pounds each. They dragged us across the yard now when we caught them. They were too big to manage any more.

Dad visited Robinson at his store. Robinson prepared deer for local hunters and had a big meat locker in the back. Dad asked him if he'd butcher the hogs on halves.

Robinson arrived with a pickup truck and a rifle. We stayed inside, but were fully aware of what was happening. Two loud reports and it was done. He loaded the hogs into the pickup. We kids didn't cry— we'd become annoyed at being dragged all around the yard, and a little scared of them. And the meat would be a welcome change. Mother cried a little.

Three days later, we stopped by the store. Dad had already purchased one of his ice cream freezers to keep the meat in. Dad arranged for the delivery. I was surprised at how much meat we got. A hundred pounds of pork loin, pork chops, and sausage spiced with red pepper flakes and sage. And bacon.

Today, there is bacon-flavored everything. I'm perfecting a bacon-flavored bacon myself.

46

GO GET WOOD

We burned a lot of wood when I was young. Until I was twelve, I thought my Indian name was, "Go Get Wood." We were each given chores to help out and teach responsibility. Sometimes we even got a small allowance for the labor, maybe twenty-five cents a week (enough for a soda and a candy bar). From the time I could walk, my primary chore was emptying the chamber pot into the outhouse every morning. Once Jake and I got big enough, we were given the task of feeding the stove and fireplace. Too small to split large logs, we would cut smaller poles, limb them, and drag the poles back to the house to slice up with the bow saw. It was hard work for twelve- and thirteen-year olds. We eventually rebelled.

By the time we had moved to the farm country on an old Macadam road that wound out of Monroe, across Snow's Mill and on to Athens, we had retired our old wood stove. The chimney at the 1840s farmhouse we rented was not set up for one, anyway. We used a hundred-pound propane bottle for cooking, a cylinder about five feet high that we had to load into the car once a month to refill. Two fireplaces provided the only heat in the old house.

The fireplace only helped a little in that drafty house. Franklin invented his wood stove for a reason—most of the heat of a fireplace goes straight up the chimney. Since the bedroom Jake and I shared was on the far end of the house, only our electric blankets prevented us freezing to death in our sleep. It wasn't unusual for a full glass of water to freeze solid next to my bedside.

It was a two-story, with inside wall planks as wide as twenty-two inches. Most of the inside had never been painted. If you peeked at the correct angle, you could see daylight when you looked into the cracks between the wallboards, right past the angled clapboards on the outside. Insulation hadn't been an option in 1840, and the only upgrade to the house had been the addition of a well pump that served the farmhouse sink—the porcelain kind with a drain board molded into it. The kitchen had a walk-in pantry, some wooden pegs for pots and pans, and no overhead cabinets. It feels odd today to walk into a square kitchen without overhead cabinets, or a square bedroom that has no closet. But when it was built, people kept their few possessions in stand-up furniture.

My Dad had been working as a bread delivery driver for a while, often a hundred hours a week. In the late spring he told us he'd have to continue those long hours, and he emphasized the importance of laying in the firewood.

We, however, rebelled. Both of us had worked 40-hour jobs the previous summer, giving over all except the first paycheck to keep the family fed. We expected the same this year. We felt we were doing enough. When we told Dad we wouldn't cut the firewood, he was surprisingly calm. "You'll cut it when you're cold enough."

We had almost no firewood on hand when it sleeted. Sleeted almost knee deep. It stayed on the ground nearly a week. School was cancelled. Nothing moved. Even the deer and rabbits called in sick. When the last fire was about six inches high, we got cold enough. We dressed in layers and dragged the bow saw and axe into the woods behind the house. It was wet. It was cold. The wind just absorbed more cold as it swept across the shiny field of ice pellets. We cut enough poles to get by for a while. Once the ice melted, we laid in a small reserve; then it sleeted again, this time about eight inches. It was a weird weather year, the year of the big tornado outbreak that sucked the pavement right off the road on the opposite side of Turkey Mountain.

The following spring, Jake and I agreed to start early laying in firewood. We sweated and sawed until we were sore and blistered. We were fairly cheerful about it, knowing that we'd get ahead of the work and have a big woodpile. We wouldn't have to go into the cold woods this winter.

We were self-satisfied with a pretty decent stack when Mother surprised Dad on his birthday. She presented him with a brand-new chainsaw. Dad and my Uncle Bert used it to cut a lot of firewood out of bigger logs than Jake and I could have ever handled.

Before fall had set in good, we moved to town. I was frustrated and disappointed to leave that big stack of firewood behind. We wouldn't have much use for the chainsaw at the new place--an 1870s house on a big lot in Monroe that had gas heat.

We learned three lessons: that self-sufficiency really was essential; that no one was cutting that wood for us; and that timing is everything.

47

WE GO FISHING

We spent many hours having dirt clod fights in Pawpaw's fields. They stuck together just enough to launch at your opponent and disintegrated upon impact with a cloud of dust. They only hurt occasionally, when one arrived that had a rock encased in it. I never thought that this skill would be useful, but it saved our bacon one chilly morning in Jones' Woods.

All I know about the Jones plantation between Athens and Monroe is that it's old. The huge house is attractive, with a dirt drive circling in front of the house. Dad took us out there a couple of times just to look at the front of the house, which was vacant then. We rode through the dirt roads that criss-crossed what had once been a large farming operation. The main road that ran to the house continued down the hill another half-mile to a creek. Someone had told us there were two old stone houses up the creek, but we were too wary of snakes to venture into that thick brush.

We liked to fish. We fished from the bank for bream, crappie and catfish in streams and ponds. Spring was approaching, and bluegill would be biting. We decided to fish the creek below the Jones house.

We unpacked the car near the bridge. I had a one-piece clear fiberglass rod that was just right for getting through bushes without tangling, with a cheap but effective closed reel. We carried our rods, worms and cricket basket from the road, working our way between bushes to the edge of the creek. It was late February, bright and sunny but the light breeze made the 45-degree temperature barely tolerable.

The creek had overflowed recently, washing away the leaves and depositing several inches of sand along the banks. The brush wasn't too thick, with bushes and trees spaced six or eight feet apart. The creek was narrow but several feet deep. We had seen teenagers jumping off the bridge to swim in it before. Its steep banks dropped straight down six or eight feet to the water.

I had just hooked up my first night crawler when Dad said, "Let's ease on out of here. Look at the snakes. Don't move too fast." Jake and I looked around. There were black water moccasins everywhere. They weren't moving, and I stood very still in a clear spot. The nearest snake was probably five feet away. I counted twenty-seven of them from where I stood. They hung on the bushes like sausages, two or three to a bush. They were stretched out at the base of the bigger trees. They were up in the trees, trying to soak up some sun. They were short and fat, most of them two or three feet long.

We had walked thirty or forty feet into the brush from the road. Now we stood among them. A few stirred a little. We looked for a clear path to get out of there, but snakes blocked every avenue. We quietly discussed what to do. The nearest telephone was a mile up the road, and the nearest cell phone was even farther--at least decade away. We carried neither Blackberries nor a GPS, and 911 was not yet invented. We were left to our own devices.

There seemed to be fewer snakes along the creek bank, so I picked up a dirt clod and scored a snake. He fell into the water, and the steep bank prevented him slithering back up right away. Jake and Dad joined in, making their shots count. We certainly didn't want to irritate one with a dud; we had to knock them out of the way without stirring up the others. Together, we cleared a path along the bank and reached the car. It took a long three minutes.

I scored nine, all clean shots. Despite the February chill, we were sweating when we reached the car. My legs were rubbery, and Dad visibly shook. We looked down from the bridge, and there were probably two hundred knotted together. Apparently we had interrupted them as mating season was beginning. There was a wild Hollywood party of snakes going on down there.

We never did get to fish that day. We were too shaken up to try another place. We went straight home, thankful that we had survived.

48

AND YOU THOUGHT YOU
HAD A CRAPPIE DAY

There was a one-acre pond behind our place on Snow's Mill Road. It belonged to our landlord next door, but he gave us access to fish in it. His only stipulations were that we had to keep the gate closed to prevent cows wandering, and we were to tell him if we snagged a resident bass he called Old Bill he had been stalking for years.

It was unusual for the entire family to go fishing, but one day we all went over to the pond with fresh cane poles and plastic bobbers to try for bream and catfish. It was warm out, but not hot. It was nice fishing weather: bright sun and just a light breeze.

We strung out along the shore. I was assigned the task of watching young Rachael. She was a cute redheaded kid, about five at the time. We took a spot next to a scraggly pine whose roots were partially exposed in the bank. You couldn't tell how deep the dark water was, but I aimed my float at a spot about fifteen feet out—as far as I could fling it with a cane pole. Rachael was too short to swing a pole, but with a serious look she put her night crawler onto a hook that was still attached to one of the plastic ladders that you bought to rig a cane pole. The ladder came wrapped in lightweight line, with the hook, line and sinker already attached. You were supposed to unwind all the line and tie it onto the end of the pole. She dropped her hook alongside the pine roots and watched it with an unusual intensity.

I flung my float out and let my mind wander a bit, while still watching my sister. The tree jutted out into the water on a little peninsula. The wind was blowing in our direction and the ripples made it feel like I was moving across the water on a boat. It was mesmerizing, but I kept an eye on Rachael. I considered what I would do if she fell in, and decided that if I couldn't catch her before she hit the water, I'd step down onto the pond bottom and hope it wasn't too deep. I was in charge of her, but neither of us could swim.

I got a couple of bites, and pulled in three or four bream, minnows really, that were too small to keep. They were maybe finger-sized. I unhooked them and sent them home to grow up. Rachel's bobber hadn't moved, but her eyes were locked on it.

I heard Rachael grunt just behind me on my right. Her line had gone taut and the weight of the fish was pulling her toward the water. I dropped my cane pole and ran toward her. She was being dragged forward. I got one hand on her shirt and barely prevented her from going over the edge.

She had a death grip on the plastic ladder. All her concentration was focused on her quarry. She'd still not said a word. I told her to sit down and pull in the line by hand, but instead, she clenched her teeth and leaned back against the strain, walking backwards away from the water.

The line didn't break. A fish emerged from the depths—a large fish. I had never caught a fish that big. I wasn't sure what kind it was. It glinted silver in the sun, and I guessed it must be a bottom-feeding carp. Those weren't much good to eat. Local lore said to prepare a carp, you had to put it on an oak cutting board; cut its throat and drain copious amounts of blood; filet down both sides of its bony skeleton, then throw the carp away and eat the cutting board. But even if it was a carp, it was an impressive fish.

By all rights the thin line should have broken before she landed it, but she got the fish onto the grass. On closer inspection, we saw that it was a crappie, the tastiest of the sunfish. But this one was different. It was so large that its normally oval body profile looked rectangular. It was a beautiful fish, silver with black speckles.

Rachael beamed and finally spoke, "I got him!" I was awestruck. I had never caught a fish half that size. It looked like it was a foot long, and it was heavy. We put it into a cooler and continued fishing for another half-hour. On the way out, we showed it to the landlord, a spry farmer of eighty-four years. He said it wasn't Old Bill the bass, but he was impressed enough to offer ten dollars for it. We politely declined and walked home.   An hour later, the landlord's son and Mr. Robinson, who ran the store just up the road, knocked on the door. They examined the fish. Almost thirteen inches. A pocket scale read more than four pounds. Both men were excited, and they offered twenty-five dollars for the fish—half a week's pay back then. Mr.

Robinson said, "It might break the state record for crappie. I'll get it mounted and display it at the store. She'll get a certificate showing it's a record."

Mother asked Rachel what she wanted to do. "It's my first fish. I'm going to eat it."

We thanked them for the generous offer, but they smiled and understood when we refused to snatch the prize from a proud five-year-old.

Even cleaned, the fish hung over the edges of a full-sized dinner plate. It served six and was delicious.

49

MEDICAL ISSUES

Getting carded to purchase hemorrhoid cream recently set me to thinking about how medicine continues to change.

When we were growing up, dental care consisted of a string tied to a doorknob or a pair of pliers in the hands of a trusted relative. A trip to the doctor was a rare event. But when you did go, medicine was handed out more freely than it is today. Some of the medication was crude and poorly understood.

A neighbor brought us head lice as a gift of their visit once. Once we realized what the problem was, the county health nurse gave us several bottles of prescription Kwell shampoo containing the pesticide Lindane that had radioactive symbols on the bottle. It got rid of the bugs. To rid patients of internal bugs, doctors dispensed large bottles of penicillin.

The bottles of penicillin contained a pink liquid that had a relatively pleasant taste. You kept it refrigerated and took it by the spoonful. It wasn't unusual to carry home a ten-ounce bottle. If you had a really bad cough, you reached for cough syrup that contained codeine.

Dad and Jake got sick when we lived in the old farmhouse outside Monroe. Both had been feverish and achy, without much appetite. The doctor sent them home with medicine for their chest congestion. They took a tablespoon each and went upstairs to sleep. It was quieter up there.

They hadn't gotten out of bed for a day and a half except to take a second dose of medicine. Mother got concerned but was not sure what to do. I didn't know, either, until I opened the refrigerator to get a drink. The bottle was larger than usual, and the green color of the liquid caught my attention. It was a twelve-ounce bottle. I read the label out of curiosity: Digitalis.

I went to find Mother. Besides being a pre-teen news junkie, I was a regular viewer of a show called *Emergency* about some Los Angeles EMTs. I remembered that Digitalis was some kind of heart medication.

Mother read the label and made haste toward the pharmacy in Monroe. The pharmacist paled when she handed him the bottle. Besides being the wrong medicine and being potentially fatal, it was a huge, expensive bottle. He called the doctor to confirm the correct prescription. The pharmacist apologized profusely and asked about their health with genuine concern.

Dad and Jake came around late that evening. When they awoke, they took the medicine for their cold. In two more days they were back to normal. There appeared to be no long-term damage. No one considered suing. We understood that mistakes happen, even among medical practitioners.

I was surprised to see a statement recently on a surgery consent form, "Surgery is not an exact science." I had been under the impression that of all things, surgery was. Even so, what is acceptable treatment today will likely be banned next year, and some new method will take its place. I guess it's live, learn, and change like anything else.

50

POTS AND PANS

I was fourteen when I bought my first metal detector. I'd been an avid coin collector since I was eleven. I would borrow twenty dollars from Mother and ride my bike to the bank at the other end of town, where I would ask for twenty dollars in pennies (twenty pounds). I'd sit on the curb, replacing all the Wheat pennies in the rolls with modern ones before I returned them. I amassed a nice collection that eventually half paid for my first car, an Austin-Healey Sprite that I pulled from a junkyard. When I saw my first detector advertisement in a coin book, I began saving up.

My first detector was a crude machine, and loud, but I found a lot of coins with it. It had no junk reject, so you had to dig every target. The best hunting places were around old houses, where you could figure out the old foot traffic patterns. Around the steps. By the back porch, where the ringer washer had discharged into the yard. In the driveway. Where the clothesline had been. Along the trail to the outhouse.

I found quite a few Buffalo nickels, silver Mercury dimes and all kinds of lost tools. But it puzzled me that I would occasionally find a frying pan, cook pot or cookie sheet deep in the ground behind a house. The ravages of time would eat rust holes through them, but a thick black gunk still clung to their inside, outliving even the metal. I didn't find these in a trash dump, but as lone signals in the middle of nowhere in the yard.

It was several years before I figured it out, and the solution to the mystery came by accident. Some of the women in the family were snapping beans while they discussed learning to cook. One of them laughed at her own early efforts, "…and I burned it so bad, I had to bury the pan!"

Suddenly those finds had a lot more personality, and would bring a smile when I found one. They still bring a smile, and are among my most special finds.

51

SNEAKING OUT

When I was a young teen, we would sneak out of the big two-story house in Monroe. We didn't get into much—there wasn't much to get into. The one pool hall was unattractive because of the sort of people who hung out there. Every store and gas station closed at suppertime. Monroe had long since closed its bowling alley and turned it into an electrical supply store. They closed the skating rink. The walk-in movie was boarded up. Monroe had a reputation for closing down any leisure activity that would cause kids to congregate, prodding the ones who had transportation to "go parking" on the dirt trails behind Deere Acres, an experimental farm on the edge of town, or to hang out in parking lots.

We didn't get into serious mischief, but Jake learned a hard lesson once. Several friends decided to go "streaking" and goaded him into joining. They picked the main residential avenue of Church Street but were timid enough to choose one o'clock in the morning so they wouldn't be caught, or even seen. They talked Jake into going first. I trailed behind, too shy and too chilly to actually get nekkid. Just as Jake got all his clothes off, approaching headlights spooked him. He sprinted down several front yards along Church Street toward his friend Raymond's clubhouse. He had too much momentum to avoid the roses.

The neat cottage-style house had an arbor perpendicular to the street; just a narrow frame eight or ten feet high, and it was wide—probably ten feet. It was like a picture frame filled with rose vines. In his haste, Jake ran right through the foot-thick rose arbor. He reached the safety of Raymond's place, and we caught up to him with his clothes. Jake looked liked he'd visited the Little Shop of Horrors and been spat out. Everywhere his clothes touched him would hurt for days.

Even if there wasn't much to do, it was a challenge to sneak out without being detected. I would ease out my bedroom window and onto the back porch roof. With minimal difficulty, I sat down and swung my legs over the edge, grasping the post holding up the porch roof. Then I'd slide down the post. It was only eight feet off the ground. Jake got more creative. His room faced another direction, and he'd reach out his window and shinny down a small cherry tree. It worked until Dad cut down the tree. Jake improvised and got caught trying to escape by dangling from the upstairs windowsill, then wedging his hands and feet mountaineer-style against the window frame of the window directly below—my parents' bedroom window frame. It wasn't a well-conceived plan.

We'd slip off to a playground two blocks up the street and hang out with a few neighbor kids, getting dizzy on the merry-go-round and such. Or we'd visit George across the street. They had a privet forest behind their house and we'd build a campfire and talk.

It all came to an end late one night. A brother of Doris' boyfriend was a longhaired guy who was a drummer in a band. Sometimes he even got professional gigs. He was the only professional musician we knew, and we were fairly impressed. We'd heard they were going to throw a party and jam with an older brother of one of Jake's friends who lived in public housing behind the jail.

We slipped out quietly and made our way up to the park that adjoined the armory and the projects. Once we heard the music start, we moved closer. We didn't go in, because they might be doing things at the party we didn't want to get involved in. We were too young for their crowd anyway. We just wanted to hear the band.

I don't know how Mother knew we'd left. She quietly got up, closed the front door and used all one hundred pounds of her small frame to push our old '63 Falcon out of the driveway. She started it and drove up to retrieve us. She was mad as a hornet.

We saw the black Falcon approaching and hid, laying low in a ditch. It wasn't as dark as we had thought, and she grabbed each of us by an ear and put us into the car.

We were apprehensive when Mother called us all together a few days later. We didn't get into trouble over sneaking out. She didn't tell Dad, either. She presented each of us with a key to the house. I was stunned. "You can come and go. You're sneaking out anyway. Just let us know where you're going. We worry about you."

It was the end of our fun. The challenge of sneaking out had been the primary fun in the first place, and Mother understood it. She had spies who would stop by the house and tell her of our activities, anyway. Adults stuck together back then. Sometimes it was a policeman—she knew most of them by name. Other times it was a neighbor or someone we did business with. If someone saw us doing something we weren't supposed to do or hanging out with the wrong kids, she knew it before we'd even returned home. All without a telephone, much less a cell phone.

52

SAFETY FIRST

Helicopter parents are a pet peeve of mine. You know the ones who hover to prevent a speck of dirt ever reaching their snowflake--the ones who call for Life-Flight when their kid scrapes a knee. We were a lot less insulated, especially growing up in the country. Bruises, scrapes and scabs on a child were not questioned by anyone. They were a rite of passage. The freedom to explore, test our limitations, and learn from failure made us stronger, and we earned self-confidence rather than self-esteem. The band Fear Like Us says it well: *Scars are Tattoos with Better Stories.*

When we lived on the farm, we'd take old metal roller skates and make skateboards that were uninspected by any government agency and ride them without helmets. You used two front sections, since the heel lip on the back sections made those unsuitable. The engineering required a skate key (ask your locksmith for one) to separate the halves of the skate, a scrap one by six, and some screws. We built some good quality boards but seldom used them. The dirt driveway was sandy on the flats were it met the road, and it climbed a moderate slope covered in sharp gravels as it approached the house. Really sharp gravels.

Tire swings were cheap entertainment. We'd spin each other until we got dizzy. I was dumb enough to take a "tire ride" just once. When the tire swing rope broke, we took turns sitting inside the tire while the others rolled it down a steep hill. Nothing makes you quite as dizzy.

We played Lawn Darts. They looked like oversized target darts, but about a foot long. The target was a hoop you laid on the ground. They were safe enough unless the person designated to retrieve them strayed too close to the target.

We swam in farm ponds without getting a water quality test. We cut down saplings with sharp axes and dammed the creek, packing unsanitary mud into the cracks. Then we swam in it. We chopped big vines loose with machetes and swung on them until they worked loose from the trees and we fell to the ground. We dusted ourselves off.

We lived outside all summer, barefoot, even in the woods; and shirtless, even when going to the store--without sun block. By the end of summer, I could crush a lit cigarette with my heel painlessly. Kids were largely treated as genderless, both among our playgroups and by adults. Girls grudgingly wore shirts in summer once they turned ten or eleven. No one thought twice about it—kids were just kids. It did break down barriers and built camaraderie between the boys and girls. We were equals.

We survived wood-burning kits hot enough to engrave elaborate designs into scrap wood. We mixed chemicals from chemistry sets. We carried pocketknives to cut kite string and brush. We usually had a box of wooden matches to light campfires.

I went to third grade in an old granite block school in Youth, Georgia that was built in the Thirties. No one blinked if you came barefoot, though I seldom did. No one was sent home for picking their fingernails or sharpening their pencils with a penknife. A classmate did cross a line when he brought his father's unloaded Luger for show-and-tell. I was concerned enough to tell the teacher, who collected it, showed it to the class for him and had his mother pick it up at the end of the day with a serious warning never to do it again.

The normal progression to manhood began with making sling shots at age six or seven out of inner tubes and Y-shaped branches. From there, you graduated to a BB gun. If you didn't mess that up, you were handed a .22 caliber single-shot rifle when you turned twelve, but you got plenty of firearms safety instruction with it. We rose to the responsibility expected of us. Serious injuries were actually quite rare and no one ever put an eye out.

I suppose there are reasons that many of these things changed. Neighborhoods got more congested. People demanded sweeping changes in response to a fairly small number of tragic injuries. But we've lost something important in child development that built stronger adults. We were allowed to make mistakes, and we were expected to learn from them. My grandfather's favorite saying was, "Did you learn something from that?" We were held accountable: not only by our parents, but also by any adult who saw us doing something wrong or seriously unsafe. Neighbors were not only allowed to correct an errant child, it was expected of them. There was a commonly agreed upon code of right and wrong and it was enforced.

We have lost so much.

THE BALL JAR
By C. D. Bonner

The Ball jar lay
broken,
Empty, dusty and devoid of the cool liquor
That once burned the throat of some silent man.
I step softly past, lest my heel
Breathe warm wet life into its upturned neck
Once again.

Made in the USA
Charleston, SC
22 November 2012